Francisco Arias

The Charity Of Jesus Christ

Francisco Arias

The Charity Of Jesus Christ

ISBN/EAN: 9783743329997

Manufactured in Europe, USA, Canada, Australia, Japa

Cover: Foto ©Lupo / pixelio.de

Manufactured and distributed by brebook publishing software (www.brebook.com)

Francisco Arias

The Charity Of Jesus Christ

THE CHARITY OF JESUS CHRIST.

BY

FRANCIS ARIAS,

OF THE SOCIETY OF JESUS.

LONDON:
St. JOSEPH'S LIBRARY,
48, SOUTH STREET, GROSVENOR SQUARE, W.
BURNS AND OATES,
PORTMAN STREET AND PATERNOSTER ROW.

1880.

PREFACE.

Born in 1533, at Seville, where also he died in 1605, having entered the Society of Jesus in his twenty-eighth year, Father Francis Arias, the author of the treatise translated in the following pages, may be said to have belonged to the first generation of the religious body founded by St. Ignatius. His life does not seem to have had many vicissitudes, but we know that he was Rector of the College of the Society at Cadiz, and that he was esteemed, while living, as a saint. He was the author of a number of works, the reputation of which was very great and widespread in his own time. The great work from which the following pages have been translated, and which is strongly recommended by St. Francis de Sales in his *Introduction to a Devout Life*, is a monument of the high aims and indefatigable industry of the theological and ascetical writers of his time. It is usually to be met with in the shape of a large folio, containing under the same cover the three separate volumes into which the whole work is divided. The title of the book in the original Spanish seems to have been simply, *Of the Imitation of Jesus Christ*. It is well known that, in the time of St. Ignatius, the book which we now know by the name of the *Imitation of Christ*, the immortal work of Thomas á Kempis, was commonly called by the title of the *Liber de Contemptu Mundi.* The work of Father Arias is called, in the translations in which it is now commonly known, by the second title of the original, *Thesaurus Inexhaustus Bonorum quæ in Christo habemus.* The three volumes are divided as follows. In the first we have a number of treatises on the titles of our Lord. He is set before us as our God, our Redeemer, our King, our Saviour, our Mediator, our Advocate, our Leader, our Priest and Sacrifice, our Teacher, Legislator, Master, and Pastor, our Light, our Life, and our Judge. The second volume puts before us, first a treatise on virtues in general, and then a series of treatises on the Christian virtues, Faith, Hope, Charity, Benignity, Mercy, Religion, Humility, Patience. The third volume contains the virtues of Prudence, Justice, Obedience, Fortitude, Temperance, Chastity, Poverty, and Simplicity. It concludes with a treatise on the Heinousness of Mortal Sin.

The characteristic of the writings of this famous author seems to be his combination of theological depth and accuracy with the tenderest piety. We are told that he was for some time a professor of theology, and every page of these treatises bears witness to the benefit which he must have derived, as an author and as a preacher, from the training of the theological chair. At the same time it must be noted that the original title of his work, *The Imitation of Christ*, is in one sense more fully deserved by it than by the work of Thomas á

Kempis itself. That is, Father Francis Arias never loses sight of our Lord and His example and teaching, and shows a familiarity with the details of the Gospel history which is remarkable even among the best ascetical writers of the Church. His work is a perfect treatise on the life of our Lord considered as our example, and, in respect of this intimate knowledge of the Gospels, he rises far above any modern writer who can be named as having written on the Christian virtues. Many of his illustrations of the example of our Lord will be found to throw a new and beautiful light on the Gospel narratives.

The present specimen of this great work has been now published, not only with the desire of increasing the number of standard spiritual books in the English language, but also with a hope that its reception may be such as to encourage those who have had charge of the translation, to proceed further in the work of making known to English readers the immense treasures of spirituality which at present lie hidden and almost unknown, except to scholars, in the glorious folios and quartos of the sixteenth and seventeenth centuries. It can hardly be thought any disparagement to the writers of an age like our own, however brilliant their abilities and however sincere their devotion, to say that they must of necessity, in most cases, lack the solid theological learning, the deep thought and concentration, and even the vigorous industry, of the men of the age of St. Ignatius and St. Teresa. However this may be, it may not, perhaps, prove a fallacious hope, that Catholics of the times in which we live may be glad to become better acquainted with these great writers, who were in old times the supports and guides of Christian faith and devotion, in that intelligent study of the great truths of our religion which seems to have been so much more common in former generations than in the nineteenth century.

H. J. C.

*London, Feast of the Purification
of our Blessed Lady, 1880.*

CONTENTS.

	PAGE
CHAPTER I.—What Charity is, and how great its dignity and value	1
CHAPTER II.—How a man should dispose himself to acquire Charity through the Divine help, and how God infuses it according to His own Divine will	4
CHAPTER III.—What constitutes the love of God, and how He is to be loved principally for His own sake, and above all things	7
CHAPTER IV.—What it is to love God with our whole heart, and what are the three degrees of this love	12
CHAPTER V.—The greatness of the benefit conferred on us by God in thus commanding us to love Him	16
CHAPTER VI.—The chief motive that should move us to love God as we ought, is the love with which God Himself seeks us, and has sought us from all eternity	19
CHAPTER VII.—That God, besides loving us, delights in us; and that we should practise the love which we owe Him by, in our turn, delighting in Him	24
CHAPTER VIII.—On the greatness of the Divine love as manifested in the mystery of the Incarnation, through which God has so fully communicated Himself to man	29
CHAPTER IX.—The greatness of this love is still more clearly manifested by the unworthiness of the person beloved	33
CHAPTER X.—The love which the Son of God shows to us in His Nativity, Circumcision, and Name of Jesus	36
CHAPTER XI.—Other proofs which Christ has given of His love for man, in calling all to His friendship and bestowing on them the Kingdom of Heaven	42
CHAPTER XII.—The signs of this love which Christ gave His disciples at the Last Supper, in washing their feet, and in instituting the Most Holy Sacrament of the Altar	46
CHAPTER XIII.—Of Christ's union, through the Blessed Sacrament, with the soul, and the fresh proof which this gives to us of His love	49
CHAPTER XIV.—The love which Christ manifested in His sermon after the Last Supper	53

CHAPTER XV.—Of the love which Christ manifested in His Passion, and which He signified in the thirst, caused by His desire to save us and to suffer for us 55

CHAPTER XVI.—Of the love of Christ in refusing all sensible consolation during His torments on the Cross 58

CHAPTER XVII.—On the love manifested by Christ after His Resurrection, in the Wounds of His Sacred Body, and in His appearances when risen from the dead 61

CHAPTER XVIII.—On the means by which Christ taught us the nature of the love which we should bear towards God, and on that which constitutes the love of friendship 65

CHAPTER XIX.—Examples, by help of which Christ has taught us this love 68

CHAPTER XX.—How we are to exercise the love of complacency and benevolence towards God. Examples of this love given us by our Lord 72

CHAPTER XXI.—Further examples of the same love of complacency . 76

CHAPTER XXII.—Of the care and study with which the Christian should strive to acquire the love of God, and of the effects which this love works in his soul 79

CHAPTER XXIII.—On the means by which we should procure this love of God, seeking it, desiring it, and eliciting it from all creatures and from all good works 85

CHAPTER XXIV.—How we ought to learn the love of God from the consideration of Divine things themselves 89

CHAPTER XXV.—On the love of charity which we owe to our neighbour, and which should be directed to the good of his soul, not to his mere temporal advantage 92

CHAPTER XXVI.—Our love to our neighbour should, especially in cases of necessity, be proved by works 98

CHAPTER XXVII.—In the commandment to love our neighbour, the goodness of God and His love towards men especially shine forth . 100

CHAPTER XXVIII.—God has shown His love to us yet more fully by the new motives for loving one another which He has given us in the Evangelical law 104

CHAPTER XXIX.—Examples, by which Christ has taught us the love of our neighbour, infusing that love into all who come to Him and believe in Him 108

CHAPTER XXX.—A particular example given to us by Christ of honouring our neighbour on festive occasions 112

CHAPTER XXXI.—An example set us by Christ of helping our neighbours in their necessities 113

CHAPTER XXXII.—Fraternal charity requires the faithful to console one another in their distresses, as we see from the examples given of our Lord 119

CONTENTS.

CHAPTER XXXIII.—In our exercise of charity to our neighbour we must necessarily bear with his faults, and must sacrifice no little of our own convenience. Examples of this in the life of Christ . . 125

CHAPTER XXXIV.—Charity towards our neighbour must be so practised, that no act performed for him is opposed to the Divine will . . 130

CHAPTER XXXV.—We ought in the spirit of charity to rejoice at the prosperity of our neighbour, as Christ teaches us by examples . . 134

CHAPTER XXXVI.—Through the charity whereby we rejoice in the good of another envy is extinguished. What this vice is, and how it may be overcome 137

CHAPTER XXXVII.—The means of acquiring the charity by which we rejoice in our neighbour's good 142

CHAPTER XXXVIII.—How our Lord through this means of desiring, not earthly, but heavenly goods, cured the tendency of His disciples to envy. His wish that all should use the same remedy against this vice 146

CHAPTER XXXIX.—The order according to which we should regulate our love of our neighbour. The extent and reasons for our love even of bad men 150

CHAPTER XL.—In what degree the good are to be more loved by us than the bad 154

CHAPTER XLI.—Other reasons why the good should be loved by us rather than the bad 158

CHAPTER XLII.—The reasons which should direct us in loving some neighbours more than others 161

CHAPTER XLIII.—Although some persons ought to be loved above others, yet in all external intercourse marks of censure and offence must be carefully avoided 165

CHAPTER XLIV.—To what extent, and for what reason, enemies should be loved, and how excellent this duty is 168

CHAPTER XLV.—Another reason which makes the love of our enemies so excellent, and so much more perfect than that of our friends . 173

CHAPTER XLVI.—In what way we ought to practise charity towards our enemies, by removing occasions of anger, and conceding our own rights in order to please them 174

CHAPTER XLVII.—Our enemies are sometimes to be propitiated by explaining to them the motive of our actions 178

CHAPTER XLVIII.—Love towards our enemies is to be preserved even while they are doing us an injury; all anger and retaliation being at once checked within us 180

CHAPTER XLIX.—How greatly it is to the interest of the Christian that he should never retaliate an injury received 184

CHAPTER L.—We must fully forgive the injury done us by a neighbour, because charity requires this of us 187

CHAPTER LI.—It does not become those who have suffered an injury, to desire its punishment on the ground of justice, even for a good end . . 191

CHAPTER LII.—We have no right to rejoice in the misfortunes of an enemy, but should feel for and commiserate him 194

CHAPTER LIII.—We should not cause even shame or vexation to our enemies by way of slight retaliation, but be ready always to console them 198

CHAPTER LIV.—We should continue our good offices of charity towards a neighbour, even though we receive but small signs of friendship in return 200

CHAPTER LV.—That we may avoid scandal, a former friend is still to be spoken to and saluted, as though he had not become our enemy 205

CHAPTER LVI.—How we are to exercise towards an enemy the especial charity of conferring benefits on him, and how Christ teaches us to do so by His own example 211

CHAPTER LVII.—It behoves us to do good to our enemies in return for the benefit they do us by showing to us our faults and by helping us to correct them 218

CHAPTER I.

What Charity is, and how great its dignity and value.

CHARITY is a virtue of the soul infused by God, by which man loves God as that particular object and final end, in the vision and love of which his happiness consists; and he loves God for His own sake, and loves himself and his neighbour for the sake of God. This is the chief and highest, the mother and queen of all virtues, since, as we have elsewhere said, amongst virtues the theological stand first, because practised towards God Himself, and of these virtues charity is at the head. For faith is directed to God as the source from which comes to man the knowledge of that truth which he is bound to believe. And hope is directed towards God as that Supreme Creator from Whom his happiness proceeds. But charity is directed to God by resting in Him and loving Him for His own sake. Hence the Apostle says: "*Now*," during this life, "*there remain faith, hope, charity.*"* And again he exhorts the faithful to seek and procure this virtue with the greatest possible diligence, bidding them, since the gifts which God bestows upon His faithful are so many and so various, "*be zealous,*" seek with desire, with diligence, and with real affection, "*for the better gifts,*" those more conducive to spiritual good. Then among these he would have them choose out and labour still more after the best, saying, "*And I show unto you a yet more excellent way,*"†

* 1 Cor. xiii. 13.   † 1 Cor. xii. 31.

meaning another gift, by help of which God and His glory are still better attained, the virtue namely of Charity and Divine love.

Charity is also the mother of all virtues, inasmuch as she brings forth, nourishes, trains, increases, and leads them on to their due perfection. This she does by a strong desire and thirst after her last end, which is God and her own beatitude; and seeing with the eye of faith that all other virtues are necessary for obtaining that end, she conceives within herself a most vehement and efficacious desire of them also, and through this produces every act of those virtues. Thus, like a mother, does she conceive and give them birth, since without her they could not help man towards his supernatural end, the beatific vision of God. Being in themselves incomplete, they are called virtues not absolutely, but with the limitation of imperfect, moral, and human; but charity, by directing and empowering them to help man towards his last end, gives them the life and substance of true and perfect virtues. This the Apostle signifies when he prays God to grant the faithful: "*that Christ may dwell by faith in their hearts,*" and that, at the same time, Christ may be "*rooted and founded in charity.*" Thus he calls charity the foundation and root of the spiritual life, not as its material part, but as nourishing it like a root and sustaining it like a foundation, and in this manner being the mother of the virtues which constitute it.

Charity is also the life and mother of other virtues, because without her they have no value or merit before God, for this can come only through Christ, with Whom they cannot of themselves join us in living membership. But when once informed by that charity which unites man to Christ, and makes man a partaker of His merits, every act of virtue becomes of the highest dignity and merit with God, and on the title of justice conduces to the end of eternal happiness. This the Apostle indicates in the words, "*If I should have prophecy, and should know all* *mysteries and all knowledge,*" that is, all Divine secrets and human sciences, "*and if I should have all faith,*" both that by which revealed truths are believed and through which miracles are wrought, and have it so perfectly that "*I could remove mountains, and have not charity, I am nothing,*" nothing as to that spiritual grace which alone makes a man of any value before God. "*And if I should distribute all my goods to feed the poor, and if I should deliver my body to be burnt*"—in furtherance of the good of religion or of the state, and have not charity prompting me to the deed through love of God above all things, "*it profiteth me nothing*"* towards saving my soul or meriting for eternal life. Wherefore St. Paul again exhorts the faithful to be moved by charity in all that they do. "*Watch ye, stand fast in the faith, do manfully, and be strengthened,*" in this not trusting your own strength, but the help of God, "*Let all your works be done in charity,*" observing in everything what the love of God requires, and having God Himself for your end.

Charity is also the queen of all virtues, for she exercises sway over all, and through this moves them to act. She directs justice to render to every one his own, prudence to be guided by reason in all actions, fortitude to overcome human fear, temperance to be content with that which is necessary for life. The actions which a particular virtue performs for its own ends, she bids it do for God, and thus changes them into acts of love to Him by making every interior or exterior good action immediately proceeding from the particular virtue of which it is the act to be an act also of the charity which controls it, and directs it towards the final end of serving and enjoying God. Whence the Apostle proceeds: "*Charity is patient, is kind; charity envieth not, is not puffed up, is not ambitious,*" &c.† And he says in another place: "*The end of the commandment is charity from a pure heart, and a good conscience, and an unfeigned faith.*"‡ Because all

* 1 Cor. xiii. 2, 3.   † 1 Cor. xiii. 4, 5.   ‡ 1 Tim. i. 5.

precepts are directed towards the fulfilment of that which charity commands and directs, and she in turn gives to them their true complement and perfection.

CHAPTER II.

How a man should dispose himself to acquire charity through the Divine help, and how God infuses it according to His own Divine will.

SINCE, on the one hand, charity is so high a virtue, and guides man to so supernatural an end as the clear vision of God, and, on the other hand, man is so weak and so inclined to the gratification of his senses, he can acquire neither the virtue of charity itself nor the dispositions necessary towards it by all his natural powers taken together; nor can anything he does through his natural strength bear any proportion to charity, which belongs to the order of supernatural and Divine truths. Thus the only author of charity is God. It is He who gives it existence, and of His free act infuses it into the hearts of those who have it not. To this the Apostle bears witness: "*The charity of God,*" which is the gift of God, and by which we love God, "*is poured forth in our hearts by the Holy Ghost,*" and through it the same Holy Ghost "*is given to us,*" and dwells within us.* Whence we see that charity is not given according to the natural faculty and virtue of any man, but according to the most gracious and liberal good pleasure of the Holy Spirit. For though man disposes himself towards the reception of charity by grief over his sins, by the purpose of fulfilling the Divine law, and by other good desires and exterior and interior good works, and though God bestows charity upon each one in proportion to his dispositions, yet, since this disposition is not man's own doing, nor the fruit of any natural faculty

* Romans v 5.

within him, but is a supernatural favour from God exciting and moving him to action, and a grace from God whereby He goes before man's action, giving him holy inspirations, and enabling him freely and readily to admit them, so the infusion of charity is attributed to God alone, Who bestows the disposition, and then, in accordance with that, the gift of charity itself.

Thus St. Paul says of the various gifts which the Holy Ghost confers on the faithful, "*All these things one and the same Spirit worketh,*" the true God "*dividing to every one according as He will.*"* But man, thus helped and moved by God, and anticipated in action by His grace, does not correspond with his best exertion or natural strength. The angels, helped in the same way by grace freely given according to each one's natural powers, being purely spiritual and intelligent creatures, work with their fullest strength and power; and so, although not even these acquire charity, grace, or glory by their natural strength, yet these gifts are bestowed on them in proportion to the natural perfection of each one. Whereas men often strive with less effort after virtue the greater their natural abilities are, because of the obstacles arising from the bodily part of their compound nature; and therefore even when, assisted by the favour of God, they readily dispose themselves for the gift of charity, yet this is never bestowed on them according to the proportion of each one's natural capacity, but according to the will of God, Who Himself has bestowed both the dispositions and charity itself.

And here it is worthy of especial note that in speaking of the infusion of charity and grace we distinguish between what is done on the part of God, and what on the part of man, saying that man disposes himself, and that God gives him both grace and charity in proportion to his disposition; while we also say that if man does all he can by preparing himself for God's gifts and striving after them, then God will act liberally to him in communicating to

* 1 Cor. xii. 11.

him His gifts, graces, and virtues. A distinction which is made, not in order to reckon up and put on one side what is done by God, and on the other what the natural power and faculty of man do, but in order to mark out what is the work of God alone, namely, charity and the creation of grace along with its infusion into the soul, and what is the work of God, as First Cause and Chief Author of nature and grace, and at the same time, of man, as God's instrument, whose it is to dispose and prepare himself to receive grace ; and though this is the work of God going before and moving man, and working through him, it is also the work of man, who of his own accord readily cooperates with God.

One object of this distinction is to stir us up to make good use of the gifts of God, and to draw full fruit from His inspirations by our readiness to receive them, and from His favours by our cooperation with them ; allowing in ourselves neither laziness nor neglect. Another object is to teach us to Whom it is that we owe the charity, the grace, the good dispositions, the supernatural gifts which help us towards our beatitude—namely, to God alone, and in no respect either to ourselves or to our natural qualities. This convinces us that we dare not be proud or presumptuous, but must humble and despise ourselves, giving all the glory to God. Without reservation, then, we declare that the whole of this is the gift and work of God.

The same holy plan the Apostle employs when exhorting the faithful to the utmost diligence in worshipping God and making good use of His gifts, *"Follow peace with all men and holiness, without which no man shall see God; looking diligently lest any man be wanting to the grace of God."** And then again to remind them of their duty to practise that humility which neither attributes anything to themselves nor seeks any honour for themselves, but ascribes all to God, he concludes : *"It is God Who worketh in you, both to will and to accomplish, according to His good will."*†

* Heb. xii. 14, 15.   † Philipp. ii. 13.

CHAPTER III.

What constitutes the love of God, and how He is to be loved principally for His own sake, and above all things.

THE virtue and habit of charity comprises two principal acts, the love of God, and the love of our neighbour on account of God. We shall treat now of the first and chief of these, which is the love of God. As charity is the highest, best, and most necessary of all virtues, so the love of God is amongst all the operations of man the most excellent and the most necessary; and it is preeminently due to God. Hence the commandment to love God is, as Christ said, "*the greatest*," and in dignity and excellence it is "*the first commandment.*"* How then is man to fulfil this precept of loving God? In the first place God must be loved as being "*He Who is.*" For God is the last end of man, so that man may not love Him for any other end, but simply for Himself. God is infinite being, whence all existence is derived; He is the infinite good, through Whom and from Whom all good proceeds.

In order to understand Who God is, let a man place before His mind some Being of most excellent nature, goodness, power, wisdom, sweetness, and beauty, and let him go on conceiving of a God still more perfect in every way than the last, repeating this thought, if it were possible, for all eternity, and after the most perfect conception imaginable, he would still be obliged to confess that God is infinitely more powerful, excellent, wise, loving, and beautiful. On this account, therefore, should man love God because He is God, and is in every perfection as infinite as God must be. And this is the true love of

* St. Matt. xxii. 38.

charity and friendship, because charity is friendship between God and man, consisting in this, that as God loves man because of His own goodness, so man loves God as being God. It is both a lawful and most excellent thing to love God because it is useful to us, and most sweet and pleasant by reason of the eternal glory and reward which we hope for from Him; since, therefore, God has created and redeemed us for the sake of our eternal happiness, it is good and lawful for us to desire that happiness, and to employ all the means necessary for acquiring it. Now of these means, one is the love of God, and so to direct our love of God to the acquisition of this end is a thing most reasonable, as Holy Scripture and the Church teach us.

We must well observe this, however, that the love of God which looks only for reward is ungenerous, and is called mercenary, or the love of concupiscence; it is also imperfect, and does not satisfy the requirements of true love. Hence it does not suffice for salvation unless the Sacrament of Penance, or some other mode of conferring grace on one truly penitent for his sins, and having a firm purpose of never again offending God, supplies its deficiency, which it does even though the motive and end of such attrition be simply to escape the pains of Hell or obtain the happiness of Heaven.

But when the servant of God worships and loves Him, because God is what He is, with the love, that is, of friendship; and at the same time loves Him for the sake of the reward of beatitude which He hopes to receive from Him, such love is neither illiberal nor mercenary, nor one that proceeds only from concupiscence. Since out of that very strong love wherewith the soul is borne towards God, as being God, springs the very strong desire which it feels of seeing and enjoying Him. For if he who bears especial love towards another man as his friend, from the motive of friendship and not of self-interest, desires much both to see and hold communication with him; how much more should he, who loves so great a friend as God is, feel a most ardent desire of the clear vision, possession, and enjoyment of Him, and apply his whole mind to the attainment of this highest good, and use every possible effort to secure it.

Besides this, the true servant of God, knowing well that when he enters upon the vision and possession of God in Heaven, he will love, praise, and glorify Him far more perfectly than he does here on earth, on that very account desires to see and enjoy God, and directs all His good works and his love to that end. And though in this desire he is moved by considerations of good to himself, he is moved far more by the thought of the greater glory that will redound to God. "For if," as St. Augustine exclaims, "we love God here on earth, when we do not see Him, how much shall we love Him when we come to see Him."* It is clear that our love will then be ineffably greater, and such shall be the praise and glory that will be rendered to Him in eternity; hence, too, a love directed to that end is not mercenary, but one of sincere charity and friendship.

Again, he who loves God because He is what He is, must also love Him above all things, and far more than he loves himself. And the first reason of this is because, as the creature of God, all that he himself is, whether in respect of nature or grace, he has received from God, whence he is bound to think more highly of God than of himself, since he belongs more to God than to himself, and should in everything prefer the will of God to his own, and the affection of God to his own self-love, having everything from God; and in this way he loves God more than he does himself. A second reason is, that he who is but a part is bound to love the good common to the whole of which he is part, more than the good which is peculiar to himself alone. Thus we see the hand, according to nature, loves the whole body more than it does itself, since

* St. Augustine, Psalm ix. 15.

it exposes itself to be cut off for the sake of the head and the rest of the body; and the citizen, if he acts according to reason, exposes himself to death to preserve the republic of which he is but a member. Each individual, therefore, as only one member of the whole republic of creatures, and especially of men capable of beatitude, is bound to love God more than himself, or than the whole universe; since it is God Who has given existence to all and preserves all, Who to the just has given all their grace and to the blessed the very existence of their glory, and possesses in Himself, with infinite excess and infinite profusion, the essence of all creatures. Thus St. Augustine: "Do you inquire how much charity we owe to a fellow-man, how much to God? To God we owe incomparably more than to ourselves, to our brother as much as to ourselves. Now we increase our love of ourselves in proportion as we increase our love of God for His own sake, and our love of our neighbour for the love of God."*

This opens out another motive for our love of God, He is not only infinite good, but He is our good; He is not only God, but He is our God. The more a thing is really his own the more does man love it. Now, nothing belongs more to man than God does, not even his life nor his essence. "*For in Him we live, and move, and are,*" says St. Paul.† He gives us our essence and our life, and He preserves these, and it is He Who both bestows on us the power to act and Who Himself acts in us. Thus Moses spoke to the people of Israel: "*Choose life,*" that is the way and the good in which life is to be found, "*that both thou and thy seed may live; and that thou mayest love the Lord thy God, and obey His voice, and adhere to Him, for He is thy life and the length of thy days.*"‡ There are two ways however in which a thing, or a good is said to belong to man. The former of these is when it is ordained for man's use, like his land, or his servant, or his wealth; and this

---

* St. Augustine, *De Trinit.* l. viii. c. 8.   † Acts xvii. 28.
‡ Deut. xxx. 19.

kind of good man does not love more than himself. The second mode is when man himself is ordained for that thing or that good, as the common good of the whole republic is said to be the good of each citizen. It is in this latter sense that God is said to be the good of man, because man is wholly ordained for God; whence though God is the portion and inheritance of man, yet man is bound to love Him incomparably more than he loves himself, for God is man's beginning and end and glory, upon Whom man is wholly dependent, and through Whom alone man lives. And this constitutes the sole happiness of man, that as he is wholly God's, so he should wholly place himself in the hands of God. This he does by giving God his whole love, according to the words of David: "*They*," that is men of the world, "*have called the people happy that hath these things*," meaning temporal things; "*but happy truly is that people whose God is the Lord,*" Whom it worships, and loves, and obeys as its God." *

* Psalm cxliii. 15.

CHAPTER IV.

What it is to love God with our whole heart, and what are the three degrees of this love.

THIS pure intention of loving God because He is God, and this height and perfection of loving Him above everything He has Himself expressed in the words that publish His precept of love. "*Hear, O Israel, the Lord our God is one Lord. Thou shalt love the Lord thy God with thy whole heart, and with thy whole soul, and with thy whole power.*" * And Christ our Lord repeating in His Gospel this same precept, adds, "*and with all thy strength, and with all thy mind.*" † By the term "*heart*" in holy Scripture is meant either the superior and spiritual part of the soul including both the understanding and the will; or else the will alone. And this last is the chief and most correct signification, the will having more sympathy with the heart which belongs to the sensitive part of man. For as the heart is the source of all the movements of the body, so the will is the source of all the interior movements of our soul. Whence in this precept it means, Thou shalt love the Lord thy God in all the desires and affections of the will, so that what thou desirest, lovest, and hopest for, shall be God Himself, God for His own sake; and whatever causes thee joy shall be the good will and pleasure of God; and whatever affects thee either with aversion or sadness shall be that which is opposed to the will of God, namely, sin. Again, the "*mind*" is used in Holy Scripture for the whole superior part of the soul, and also for the

* Deut. vi. 4.   † St. Luke x. 27.

"*understanding*" only, and this is the more frequent and correct use, and is intended in this precept. St. Mark indeed substitutes the word understanding for mind,* as being that with which man believes whatever faith teaches and the Church proposes to be believed, and for the sake of God submits in obedience to his elders and to the counsel of the wise, and occupies himself in contemplating and meditating on God, and on those truths which respect His knowledge and His love and the fulfilment of His will. The "*soul*," in its usual and correct sense, denotes that principal and spiritual part of the body which gives life to the body and to man himself. It is sometimes used for the whole compound being of man, at other times it signifies that part in which man's appetites and sensitive affections are seated, the inferior therefore and corporal, with all its passions, whether love, or hatred, or desire, fear, boldness, hope, desperation, anger, sadness, and joy. Such is the sense in which it occurs in this precept, as distinguished from the superior part of the understanding and will. It requires us to order as far as possible and with generous will all the motives and passions of our sensitive appetites to promote within us the love of God; restraining and mortifying them in everything opposed to the Divine law and the Divine will. Thus not only the intellect and will, but the whole interior action of our sensitive appetites, and the use of our exterior senses, are made to serve and obey this same love of God. Fortitude or strength in Scripture signifies, as part of this precept, that faculty in man by which he executes all his external operations, both in his own person and in the employment of his external means and property, through which he influences those who are under his power and control. These operations therefore which we exercise either in ourselves or through our external goods and position in life, or through the persons of our children and of those subject to us, are all to be directed to the love of God, and to

* St. Mark xii. 33.

be exercised for Him, and to have God as their end. Thus not our will only, which is the immediate seat of love, but also all the other faculties controlled by our will promote the love and glory of the most high God. It is then by the exercise of each and all of these powers that God wills and commands that He should be loved.

Before, however, we can understand the full force of this precept we must observe that, as the virtue of charity has its different degrees, for it is necessary in those who begin to serve God, in those who are making progress in His service, and again in those who are perfect; so also the act of charity, that is of loving God with the whole heart, has its three degrees differing in approach towards perfection. The first and lowest of these degrees is when a man gives the chief part of his heart and love to God, not admitting any affection that is opposed to charity or dividing his heart by fixing it on anything except God as its last end; though at the same time he allows some amount of inordinate affection in his heart towards many earthly things, such as wealth, advantages, or honours. This degree of love all those have who are resolved to commit no mortal sin for the sake of anything that this world can offer them; and yet they easily commit those venial sins, put in their way by the things of this world, to which their tastes and their pleasures attract them. Though this degree of love towards God suffices for actual salvation, since it really places above all other things the precept by which charity is preserved and God is loved above everything, yet it is a very weak love and does not struggle against an inordinate love for creatures. Besides which, it is exposed to great danger of extinction, for it deliberately admits venial sin which draws the soul towards the commission of mortal sin. This degree of love of God at the very least must be formed in every one beginning to love Him.

Another and more excellent love of God is that which centres man's whole love on God, abstracting it from all creatures, and directing whatever he desires, loves, and undertakes to the love of God and the fulfilment of His will. It in addition hates and flies from, not only mortal sin as opposed to charity, but also venial sins which injure it and endanger its existence. Not only does it prefer, to everything which this world can offer, obedience to the precepts that bind under mortal sin, but also every other precept of God binding under sin at all; and in all things it seeks to do the will of God, abstaining from many lawful gratifications, and observing many of the counsels of Jesus Christ, tending to increase its love of God. This second degree admits of many gradations, implying less or greater perfection, a fact which is equally true of persons advancing in any virtue, even of those who are very perfect in practising it.

There is yet a third degree of love contained within this precept, according to which the soul always and unceasingly loves God, so that what it says, does, or thinks of, and whatever inclinations or interior movements it experiences, each one springs from the actual love which it bears towards God. And this love is not only constant, but most intense, filled with all possible fortitude and strength. This degree constitutes the love of the Blessed, and has its full exercise only in Heaven, where those who see God face to face, and, without any intervening veil, contemplate His infinite goodness and beauty, always love Him with the most perfect charity, and with immense gratification and pleasure enjoy the fruition of His infinite benefits. And God has willed that in His precept of love as proposed to man on earth this degree of love should be included, in order that in the same command in which we read the love we owe to God on earth we should understand also the end towards which our love is to be directed, namely, the degree of love borne towards God in Heaven. Thus St. Augustine says, "in the fulness of charity," which we shall possess in our heavenly inheritance, "we shall fulfil the precept of loving God with our whole heart" in all perfection.*

* St. Augustine, lib. *De Perfect. Justitiæ*, c. viii.

CHAPTER V.

The greatness of the benefit conferred on us by God in thus commanding us to love Him.

IT is impossible to explain the fulness of that benefit which God has bestowed on us in commanding us to love Him with our whole hearts. Had He simply enabled and allowed us to do this the favour would have been beyond expression, for it is the nature of love to produce an affinity between him who loves and the object which he loves. If a man's affections are drawn to the things of earth, he himself becomes wholly earthly. If he loves what is impure, disgraceful, or of the nature of mortal sin, he himself becomes wholly tainted with impurity, dishonour, and deadly sin, and deserving of eternal punishment; if he loves the vanities of this world, he himself becomes vain and worthless. "*They became abominable, as those things were which they loved.*"* "*They have walked after vanity, and are become vain.*" But he who truly loves God, Most High, of infinite Majesty, Omnipotent, all wise, most glorious, of perfect beauty and sweetness, very Excellence and Holiness itself, that man becomes himself as though divine and heavenly, he attains to the highest dignity and authority in the house of God, he becomes very powerful and wise and glorious, and acquires such a wonderful beauty of soul that he rejoices Heaven, and delights God Himself by the sight; being just, holy, and the friend of God, worthy of His eternal society and of the possession

* Osee ix. 10.

of His glory. For of those who love God it is written: *"Eye hath not seen, nor ear heard, neither hath it entered into the heart of man what things God hath prepared for them that love Him."** So sublime, supernatural, and near to God are these things, that they transcend incomparably all that the creature can by the light of nature comprehend, or place distinctly before himself in his desires. Since this is the character and efficacy of love, it would certainly have been the highest favour on the part of God had He granted to man only leave and liberty to love Him. But for Him to have commanded it, and to have bound man, by the greatest of all commandments, to love Him, and nothing else but Him, and for His sake, this is a far more excellent benefit. First, because the fact that God does command, and is not satisfied with only permitting it, bears fullest testimony to the strength of His will and desire, and the value He sets on possessing man's love, on having him for a friend, and on being able to bestow on him the dignity and glory which He gives to all that love Him. Thus it is that when the Supreme Pontiff, in conferring upon some priest the dignity of an archbishopric or a cardinal's hat, does not only present it to him, but command him to receive it, that priest will esteem this as a high honour and favour, because it proves what great opinion the Holy Father has formed of him, and how desirous he is of so advancing him. Wherefore that God has commanded man to love Him as the means to attain eternal glory, and threatens eternal punishment should he refuse, is the strongest possible sign of His desire for man's love, and of the deep sorrow and offence which man's refusal causes Him.

In the second place, this command of God is a very great favour, for had He granted to man only permission to love Him, without commanding it, then man would not have felt so certain that God would bestow on him the helps and graces necessary to produce that love; for unless God had laid on him the obligation of loving, God for His

---

* 1 Cor. ii. 9.

part would have been under no obligation to bestow the necessary grace, whereas now He is. For it were unworthy of the Majesty of God to command an impossibility, but most befitting His goodness to impart every help to fulfil His precept—nay, He has by word bound Himself to this. And in addition to all this, if we will use His gifts aright He will shower down upon us yet fuller and more abundant graces, so as to render both easy and delightful to us the holy exercise of His infinite love—love of the supreme goodness, beauty, and sweetness of God. He Who is so magnanimous in all that He does and so liberal in all the gifts which He confers, will surely be all this still more fully in a matter of so great value and desire to Him as man's more perfect fulfilment of the great precept of loving Him. To bestow a gift of richest value on one who is cold and whose esteem of it is but small, or on one so worthless in himself as to be incapable of return, is a difficult and painful act, and cools all ardour in the giver. But to bestow the same on one who desires and prizes it, or on one so elevated and powerful as to accept it gladly and repay it nobly, is very easy and pleasing in execution, and enhances the gratification of giving it. Now, since love surpasses everything else that we have in us of value, and is the richest gem of all our wealth, let us not throw it away upon those earthly creatures which care little for it and are worthless in themselves, and incapable of either gratitude or recompense. But let us bestow it all on God, Who so greatly desires it, Who asks it of us with so tender affection, and Who is in Himself the Most High God, of infinite power and goodness, thankful to receive it from us and prompt to make return, loving those who love Him, and lavishing upon them all His good things and Himself also in return for love, as He also testifies: "*I love them that love Me; and they that in the morning early watch for Me shall find Me; with Me are riches and glory.*"* Nor are these inferior riches, but the noblest, most glorious riches

* Prov. viii. 17.

of *justice* or sanctity. "*I walk in the way of justice*," and make My friends to walk also: "*that I may enrich them that love Me, and may fill their treasures*" with the most precious gifts of grace and eternal glory.

CHAPTER VI.

The chief motive that should move us to love God as we ought, is the love with which God Himself seeks us, and has sought us from all eternity.

THAT point which we should observe and dwell upon in the mysteries of Christ as narrated in the Gospel, for the purpose of moving us to satisfy our obligation of loving God, is the love which God Himself has borne and still bears towards us. For, as St. Augustine says, "There is no stronger invitation to love than to anticipate another by our love. And hard indeed is that heart which shows itself unwilling to repay love, even though it refuse to love first;" more especially if it be a God, as in our case it is, Who shows Himself first to love. Since this, then, is, amongst all the benefits of God, the most powerful in moving us to love Him, we are bound to discover and weigh it well as manifested in the mysteries of Christ. For in the love of God towards us we acknowledge His goodness, and this is the principal reason why we should love Him, for it is the root and source of all the benefits He has conferred on us by which, as by live coals, the flame of love is kindled, and thus by extending His love to us God has more enriched us than by all the other favours He has granted us. For when God loves the man who loves Him, He becomes, by means of this spiritual and ineffable love, in a manner one with man and transforms man into Himself, and in a certain way remains bound, united with, and a captive to man by the voluntary and most sweet bands and chains of love.

St. John indicates the same when he says, "*He that abideth in charity,*" loving God and beloved by God, "*abideth in God, and God in him.*"* He himself remains united to God as to his highest good and last end, and as being in Him Who is his protection, safety, and glory; and God remains united to him as in His chamber where He lodges, His seat in which He rests, His garden of delights wherein He is especially refreshed; God remains with him as a most fond father with his son, or a most affectionate friend with one equally faithful to him. For this reason, namely, that in His love God unites us so closely to Himself, makes us such full sharers with Himself, joins Himself so intimately with us, giving His Heart to us and making Himself ours, it is true that however great may be all the gifts and benefits He has bestowed on us, inasmuch as they came from His own blessed hand, and are all directed to the end of our eternal happiness, yet this particular gift and benefit, His love to us, is the greatest of all, and most fully manifests His infinite love, excites most our love and influences His.

Let us, therefore, open out more the dignity and magnitude of this love. In the first place, this love of God for us never had a beginning, it is eternal, as God Himself is eternal. For as He had no beginning in Himself, so neither had He in the operations of His understanding or His will; so that from all eternity He saw and comprehended Himself, loved Himself with an infinite love, and with infinite joy delighted in Himself. And since it most entirely became His infinite goodness that He should communicate Himself to others and that there should be intelligent creatures who might know, love, and enjoy Himself, He decreed to create the angels, and man, and all the other creatures which serve man. And since in His own Divine essence He saw all men whom He was to create, so from all eternity seeing them in Himself He loved them in the same love wherewith He loved Himself

* 1 St. John iv. 16.

and His own Divinity, He loved them with an infinite love. The difference is that His love towards Himself is natural and has for its object and end that which is infinite, and takes its complacency in the infinite good, that is in Himself; whereas in loving man from all eternity, such love is free and voluntary, and though infinite in itself, yet its object, man beloved, is finite, and the good communicated by Him and from which He draws His complacency in man is finite and limited, since it is but a participation of His Divinity.

Besides this dignity possessed by the love of God as eternal, it has this further excellence of being full of kindness and liberality. An intelligent creature, such as man or the angels, cannot love another unless it sees in him some good preceding and instigating its love; but God loved man before there was in him either goodness or existence, and it was His own love that determined Him to bestow upon man existence and goodness, which accordingly in time He did. "There are two things," says St. Augustine, "for the sake of which God loves His creature, namely that it may exist, and that it may continue to exist."* And in another place: "God loves us as being that which we ought to be through His gifts, not which we are in our own deserts."† And not only has God loved us before we had any being, from no antecedent merit, or goodness, on our part; but, even knowing us to be sinners unworthy of any good thing, and even under sentence of eternal punishment, He loved us in order that He might confer on us the greatest of all His benefits, namely, His only begotten Son to be our Redemption. Hence it is not only in time that He has loved us by redeeming and saving us through the Passion and death of His Son, whilst we were sinners and enemies, which, as the Apostle observes, is the height and truth of the fulness of Divine love, "*God commendeth His charity towards us, because when as yet we were sinners He gave His only Son that according to*

---

* St. Augustine, lib. i. *in Gen.* i.   † *Idem*, lib. *De vera Innocent.*

the time He should die for us;"* but also in eternity, while already foreseeing our sins, He loved us by decreeing within Himself that He would give us His only Son to be our Saviour, at the time appointed by His Divine Providence. So beneficent, so liberal was the love with which God has followed and still follows us, antecedent to any good or merit in man.

And though it be indeed true that the merits of our Lord Jesus Christ and of all the just have preceded many effects of God's love to us and many benefits which, out of love, He has bestowed on us, (since the merits of Christ necessarily came before the justification of the sinner and all the gifts and supernatural graces conducting to that end, inasmuch as these are given in consideration of those merits); and though it be true that the merits of holy living are requisite in men of sound reason before soul and body are glorified, or increase of grace is given them, yet the first gift of Christ Himself, as the root and source of all merit, was bestowed without any antecedent merit. From all then that has been said we see that whatever gifts of nature or of grace we possess, they are all to be attributed to the most beneficent love which God has borne to us antecedently to all merit, and also to His good will and pleasure, and to His infinite goodness and mercy.

Thus St. Paul declares of the eternal Father, "*Who hath predestinated*," and from eternity constituted us "*unto the adoption of children*" of God, in this life to the possession of grace, and in the eternal life to glory as the perfected adoption of the sons of God; and all this "*through Jesus Christ*," that is, through His power and merit.† Then he adds: "*according to the purpose*" and good pleasure of His own Divine "*will*." As if he had said: the first and principal cause of this election and predestination, and of all the gifts of God has been the Divine will, because it so pleased God to act. This is the first spring and origin of all the good that God renders or will render to us, and not

---

* Romans v. 8. † Ephes. i. 5.

the dignity or merit of any creature; from this source have sprung the merits of Christ and of all just men, everything is to be attributed to this most full and tender love of God. As a mother who conceives her child, developes his life within her breast, bears him for nine months in her womb, and afterwards gives birth to and brings him forth into the light of this world, thus does God conceive us from eternity in His love, decreeing to make us His sons through grace and glory. He gives life to us in His own Divine mind by His eternal purpose and election, choosing and constituting us His sons and partakers of His Divinity. Thus conceived and generated, He has borne us through the whole of an infinite eternity that hath no beginning, within the womb of His Divinity, and the bowels of His mercy; and then, when the fit time had come, He gave birth to us and brought us forth into the light of life, grace, and glory. Those whom He had eternally conceived and begotten in His love, purpose, and eternal election, He generates in time by His Word, by His Sacraments, and by His gifts within the womb of the Church, and causes them to be born children of grace, and at length perfects them in His glory. According to this He Himself speaks to us by His Prophet: "*Shall not I, that make others to bring forth children, myself bring forth?*"[*] I shall make the Church My spouse, and she shall bring forth to Me innumerable children, men holy and just like to Me through the gift of grace and glory which I shall communicate to them.

O incomprehensible love of God! O immense fire of charity! O wonderful condescension and favour that God should thus conceive and beget us as His sons for all eternity. How justly does St. John urge us to meditate and admire this most glorious effect of love and manifestations of immense charity: "*Behold what manner of charity the Father hath bestowed upon us, that we should be called the sons of God,*"[†] and this not merely according to

---

[*] Isaias lxvi. 9.   [†] 1 St. John iii. 1.

outward seeming and title, but as being, in truth, His cherished and beloved sons; and that, as such, we should be admitted into the inheritance of His glory.

CHAPTER VII.

That God, besides loving us, delights in us; and that we should practise the love which we owe Him by, in our turn, delighting in Him.

HE who loves with ardour rejoices at the good which he sees in the object beloved; and in like manner God, Who has loved men from all eternity, eternally rejoices in their good. God draws pleasure and satisfaction from everything that He has made, as David sings: "*The Lord shall rejoice in His works;*"* since all are good, His goodness shines forth in all, and all promote His glory. But in those great works which God has wrought in the sons of men, and in the goods which He has communicated to them, He specially delights and rejoices, according to the testimony of Sophonias † thus addressing the faithful soul: "*The Lord thy God will rejoice over thee,*" and over thy spiritual and eternal well-being "*with gladness.*"

Let us briefly consider what it is which God sees in man to cause Him joy and delight. He first rejoices to see in us His own image formed again by the gifts and graces of the Holy Spirit. God created man to His image in those things which regarded his nature, and after His likeness according to the grace and the supernatural life which He gave him. Sin had deformed this image and left it degraded and corrupted, for man had lost his supernatural life and had been wounded in the natural part of his being. This image God repairs and renews by heavenly virtues and graces which He infuses into man, and now seeing this image thus adorned and ennobled He

* Psalm ciii. 31.   † Soph. iii. 17.

feels an unspeakable pleasure. Man himself rejoices to see the fair image of himself in that which is partly dead, how much more will God rejoice to see His own living image in man adorned with all that admirable beauty and sublime dignity which grace has imparted to it, since all the more does He love what is good, according to the excellence which He finds in it. Secondly, God rejoices to see Himself in our souls. In order to elevate and enrich our souls, God does not only confer His graces upon us, but He gives Himself to us, He dwells and remains with us as in His own house, and in His love abides with us as the throne and spiritual resting-place of His Divinity. When, therefore, He so much loves us, because He sees us possessors of the infinite good which He Himself is, and retaining Him within our souls, and united to Him and enriched with the treasures of His Divinity, He thence draws inconceivable joy.

Once more, God rejoices to see in us eternal felicity and glory, since by this His likeness and image are impressed much more perfectly on the soul, His greatness and beauty grow beyond expression within us, and in the state of glory God is much more completely united with the Blessed, He dwells and abides in them in a far more excellent manner, and is yet more intimately united to them by a closer and higher bond of love. Every father rejoices to see his son placed in a position of dignity; and the higher that dignity is, and the greater his love for him, by so much the more will he rejoice. But when the love of God for man is so exceeding great, and when the dignity of the glory to which man is raised is so sublime, how incomprehensible ought that joy to be that dwells in the Divine Heart at the sight of the height of dignity to which man, so beloved by Him, has attained? Such as these are the objects of God's love and of His highest gratification: "*My delights are to be with the children of men.*"*
This joy is no created thing in God, no accidental qualifi-

---

* Prov. viii. 31.

cation as in us, but it is God Himself and His actual Divine essence; it neither began in time nor had any starting-point like the joy of creatures, God from all eternity rejoiced with joy incomprehensible in those benefits that He was about to communicate to man elected to them.

From this come fresh motives for concluding how just and befitting it is that we give our whole love to God, loving Him with our whole heart according to the precept He has given us. We feel a strong affection towards some old friend who, we know, has loved us from our youth, and continues still to bear to us a love increasing with his advance in life. Nor do we less love that friend who, we know, has loved us from no self-interested motive of past or future benefits, but himself confers these and greatly rejoices in our every good. If so, how much more just that we should love God, Who, though infinite in majesty, bears to us a love that knows no beginning and is infinite, has for ever persevered in it, and was most beneficent and generous in its exercise before we ever learnt to love Him, and in our entire incapacity to confer any benefit on Him, though He has need of nothing, for there is neither in Heaven nor on earth anything that can hurt or can assist Him. And along with so wonderful a love He has communicated to us the highest gifts of grace and pledges of eternal life, and delights and rejoices ineffably in our good, with an eternal joy proceeding from pure love. "*Let us therefore love God, because God first hath loved us.*"*

In order to fulfil this precept we must in good time and with great attention meditate deeply in our hearts on the greatness and perfection of the love which God has borne to us from all eternity, on the goodness whence it flows and the benefits which it has conferred, and incited by so many motives of love we must piously resolve to fulfil His Divine will in everything, preferring it to all earthly objects, nor consciously allow within us any serious or slight fault against it, seeking in whatever we do not our own honour

* 1 St. John iv. 19.

or choice, but His good pleasure and glory. And at the end of our mental prayer let us consider that God is infinite, that His power, wisdom, goodness, and beauty are infinite, and that He derives infinite glory and happiness from the perfect knowledge and contemplation of Himself, from the fullest love wherewith He is capable of loving Himself, and from the infinite enjoyment of His own perfections.

And as God has eternally delighted Himself in those blessings which He was about to impart, and did in time impart to man, so man should with the utmost sweetness feel an abiding joy and complacency in the goods which God from eternity has possessed, and ever does and ever shall possess. He should rejoice to see God so powerful that nothing can resist Him, so wise that He sees everything, so good that He is the inexhaustible source of goodness, so blessed as to be an immeasurable abyss of all holy pleasures, and to be sweetness and meekness itself. Let him also ponder over that love with which all the Blessed love God most ardently and without end, that perpetual glory and praise which they are rendering to Him; and let him rejoice in full heartfelt joy that God is so loved and glorified in Heaven, while he prays with earnest petition to God that all still on earth may imitate the inhabitants of Heaven, knowing Him with true faith, loving Him with a most interior love, and in every respect accomplishing His Divine will. This joy and relish in the good things of God is both love and the fruit of love, wherefore it is called "*the joy of the Holy Ghost,*" and that same Holy Spirit bids us through the mouth of David, "*Delight in the Lord,*" and not in the vanities of this world. Let Him be your joy, let all your delight be in Him and for the sake of Him, and this will so please Him, that in answer to it "*He will give thee all the requests of thy heart.*"*

Happy, then, the soul which has long acquired this love

* Psalm xxxvi. 4.

of God, through which it wholly conforms itself to His will, flying everything that offends Him, rejoicing in God, uniting itself with God, and possessing God as its dwelling place, its rest, its refuge, its every good. Can there possibly be greater felicity than thus to claim as its own infinite goodness, eternal glory, superabundant joy, the heaven of all pleasures, the fount of all sweetness? With how great reason has it been said, "*All they that love Thy name, O Lord, shall glory in thee,*" in Thy power, in Thy goodness, and in all that Thou art, for they shall see and experience in very truth that Thou dost good to "*and dost bless the just,*"* enriching him with the highest and with eternal benefits.

And what we have hitherto described is that exercise of love, by which we must put into execution the commandment of love. And since, as we have been showing, the chief motive of our love of God is a living and efficacious knowledge of God's love towards us, as the strongest proof He has given of His goodness to us, I will now explain this same love in the order of the mysteries of Christ our Lord.

* Psalm v. 12.

CHAPTER VIII.

On the greatness of the Divine love as manifested in the mystery of the Incarnation, through which God has so fully communicated Himself to man.

SINCE of all the mysteries which God has wrought in the world, and of all the benefits which He has conferred on man, the greatest is that He Himself became Man, to give salvation and eternal life to man; so is it the greatest manifestation of the infinite love of God for us, for it is the especial property of love to communicate oneself, and of the most perfect love to communicate oneself in the most perfect way. And this is what God made Man has done. Nor has He given Himself to man only through His natural gifts and supernatural grace, by means of which man may to a certain extent share in His Divinity through that which is created, as grace is; but He has also communicated His very self to him, by a direct communication of His own Divinity. The Incarnation of the Son of God was nothing short of this, since in it He by direct contact united human nature to His own Person possessing the self-same Divinity as the Father, and He Who is God became Man, not by confusion of natures, but by a true and distinct human existence. Thus did God communicate Himself to man as his infinite good, in the most perfect manner conceivable; and thus did He at the same time show to us His infinite love.

It is also a property of love to unite both him who loves with the object beloved, and the object beloved with him by whom it is loved; and the greater and more intimate this union is, so much stronger is the love. But no greater nor more wonderful union could exist than for human nature to be united to the Divine Person, and that by so close a bond as to make God and Man one and the very same Person. And hence springs that second effect of love, that the person loving should make himself equal, and in every respect, as far as is possible or befitting, like to the object loved. For indeed in things that are very disproportionate and unlike, so perfect a love cannot exist as can between those in which there is some parity and resemblance. Wherefore God by assuming human nature and becoming Man, without losing in the smallest degree His own glory and majesty, made Himself like to man, and in every respect, as far as He could or ought, equal to him. Then, in order to manifest His supreme love to man in this act, He most powerfully moved that same man to love Him with his whole heart, when he saw his God made so near and so like to himself, in that human nature which He had assumed for man's sake.

In another way God showed forth His love in this mystery, for it is a very marked aim of the lover to strive in every way to centre another's love wholly on himself, and to remove from him every opportunity of loving any one besides himself, and to supply him with the strongest reasons for giving his whole love to him alone. And this again God did most perfectly in becoming man; for as man is composed of body and soul, of flesh and spirit, through sin he lost in great measure his knowledge and relish of what is spiritual and invisible, bestowing his love and affection more completely on carnal and visible things. And these things being nearer to him in likeness and equality and in his acquaintance with them, enabling him to draw greater pleasure and gratification from them, he soon came to esteem and love them, to crave them and possess himself of them. When, further, he perceived that some of these created bodies excelled himself in particular qualities and functions of their nature, as the heavens, the planets, and the elements, he was misled into such an admiration of them as to place himself in subjection to them, and adore them as deities.

Now to deliver man out of this state of abjectness and misery into which he had fallen, and cure him of so lamentable a disease, there could have been no more powerful or efficacious remedy than that human nature should be elevated by God to the sublime dignity of union with one of the Divine Persons of the Godhead, and that God should become visible and corporeal in human nature. By which means, man thus seeing himself raised to a sublime height, and recognizing in this the dignity of his nature and the noble and glorious end for which he was created, would no longer consent to remain subject to these corporeal creatures, nor to acknowledge them to be superior to himself, nor yet again to constitute them the end of his being, or the objects of his love; but on the contrary, looking on God thus become a visible and corporeal man like himself, he might through that which is visible come to know that which is invisible in God, and through what is corporeal in Him might understand His Divine spirituality and His Divine perfections; and so might raise his heart and mind to meditate on Him, might centre his whole love and affection on Him, and seek in Him alone all his rest and all his glory.

For these and other reasons which Holy Scriptures and the saints teach us, we declare and confess that this most holy mystery is the highest of all manifestations to us of the immense love of God towards man. And St. John by inspiration signified this when he said: "*God so loved the world as to give His only-begotten Son.*" *
Men were involved in complete ignorance of the love that God bore towards them, and some of the wisest amongst them, called Philosophers, held that God neither loved men, nor exercised any providence over them; others thought that He loved good men, yet they professed no certainty, but only a doubtful opinion about the matter.

* St. John iii. 16.

The chosen people of God, by help of the light of faith, and the knowledge of the Scripture, knew for certain that God loved man, but as to the greatness, the efficaciousness, or the extent of that love they were ignorant. Then came St. John the Evangelist, who flying high like the eagle and penetrating the sanctuary of the Divinity, saw with the clear eye of faith the sublime mysteries of God, the greatness of His goodness and love, and filled with the highest admiration, broke forth into the words: "*God so loved the world*," followed it with a love so immense, so strong, and so tender, "*as to give His only-begotten Son.*" God greatly loved all men, which His act of creating them fully proved, giving them both essence and life, preserving these in them, placing all His lower creatures at their service, bestowing on them the light of reason, supernatural helps, and holy inspirations, and sanctifying such as obeyed these: in fine, doing good by them to others, as Moses testifies: "*God hath loved the people, all the saints,*" just and holy people, "*are in His hands;*" all depend upon and are preserved by Him.* God loved the children of Israel especially and above all the other nations of the earth, and in testimony of this, He delivered them from Egyptian bondage by prodigies and wonderful miracles, He chose them to be His peculiar people, and through the ministry of angels He gave them a law written on tables of stone. When Moses said to them: "*The Lord thy God hath chosen thee to be His peculiar people of all peoples that live upon the earth. Not because you surpass all nations in number, hath He chosen you, but because He hath loved you,*" and hath desired to keep "*His oath, which He swore to your fathers.*"†

This love of God to man was great, and great were the proofs and testimonies to it which He gave, but far greater than this was the love with which God followed after man, and far higher than any before were the testimony and proof which He finally gave. How much more God loved

---

* Deut. xxxiii. 3. † Deut. vii. 6.

man let St. John tell us: "*God so loved the world, as to give His only-begotten Son; that whoso believeth in Him,*" with a living faith, "*may not perish, but may have life everlasting.*" Now, the rank of the person who loves throws great light on the character of his love. If he who loves is a person of high rank in the State, his love is of great value, but it is more valuable if the person be either a king, or the Supreme Pontiff, or some great saint. And should the love shown be in full proportion to the dignity or excellence of the person loving, then the higher and holier he is, the more highly shall we value the love which he bears to us. When, then, He Who loves men is God the Father, the source of Divinity, from Whom the Son is begotten, and the Holy Ghost proceeds, Who proceedeth also from the Son; and when He is infinite in majesty, in goodness, and in all perfections, and loves man according to that His infinite greatness and goodness, how immense and how incomprehensible must that love be wherewith this Lord and God the Father embraces the children of Adam!

CHAPTER IX.

The greatness of this love is still more clearly manifested by the unworthiness of the person beloved.

THE more worthless in himself and undeserving of love a person is, so much the stronger and more intense must be the feeling by which he is greatly beloved. A greater and stronger affection is necessary for loving one of worthless character, than for loving a good man; or an enemy, than a friend; or, again, a poor man who can be of no service to us, than a rich man who can repay us handsomely.

Let us now see who it is that is beloved by God. He Who loves is the Supreme Lord and Ruler of all created things, the source of Divinity. St. John tells us who are the persons beloved, "*He so loved the world.*" They were not men especially holy or god-like, not men free from sin, not friends nor faithful servants, but earthly and mortal men, worldly-minded and sinful, ungrateful to their Creator, and enemies of His eternal Majesty. The most high God loved His unworthy servant, the unchanging and everlasting God loved man who was dust and ashes. He Who is glory itself loved him who was full of miseries. Infinite goodness loved man filled with iniquity. This is He Who loved, and these are they who were loved. And although the dignity alone of the Person loving and the unworthiness of the person beloved exhibit in strong light the greatness of the love bestowed, this is proved with far greater force by the quality of the gift conferred by Him Who loves on the beloved.

What then has God our Heavenly Father bestowed on sinful men in the superabundance of His love? It is His only-begotten Son. It is not some man of peculiar sanctity, nor an angel from Heaven, but His own Son, eternally begotten of His own very substance, as powerful, as good, as wise as He Himself is, One and the same God with Himself. Whatever God might in His love have bestowed on us would have been a wondrous gift and the proof of a wondrous love, as coming from so great a God; how much more wonderful then is it, when it is actually His own Son Whom He hath given! Had the Eternal Father, the source of all Divinity, possessed many Sons, begotten not created, towards whom He felt a divided love, and had He bestowed even one of them on us, His love for us must have been extreme. But since He had one only Son, the figure of His substance, in Whom was centred His whole love and His whole delight, the most willing bestowal on us of His Son, made man and wholly devoted to our benefit and salvation, manifests a love so lofty and so profound that God Himself can alone comprehend its nature or the vastness of the excellencies stored up within it. For the Son of God is the fount of all grace and sanctity, and of all virtues; the Father then by giving Him to us, gives us in Him grace and every virtue. The Son of God is the unlimited Heir of all His Father's possessions, by giving us Him then the Father gives us with Him the inheritance of Heaven, that we may be co-heirs with Him to all the good things of God. "*By this hath the charity of God*" the Father "*appeared towards us, because God hath sent His only-begotten Son*" made man "*into the world, that,*" by the life of grace and glory, "*we may live by Him.*" *

O man, how much dost thou not owe to God the Father for this wondrous love, and for its confirmation by so wondrous a gift! How much dost thou not owe to God the Son, Who loves thee with the same love that the Father doth, since, having the self-same Divinity as the Father, He has for thee the self-same love, and confirms it with the self-same proof, inasmuch as He gave Himself wholly to man, did actually become man and expended Himself unreservedly in procuring man's salvation! O man, most blessed! so greatly beloved and esteemed of God, that though but earth and the prey of such great miseries, God hath done for thee in His love what He hath not done for the angels, those spiritual existences pure from all sin and free from every misery. O earth, most favoured! thus loved and prized and dignified by God in that He hath united thee unto Himself, not alone through the union of His Divine Person with thy soul, as a spiritual being made to His likeness, but with thy body also, formed out of the earth; so that it was said in all truth: the Eternal "*Word was made flesh.*"†

O God Most High, how immense hath been Thy love for man, for, in order to raise him above all creatures, both in his body and in his soul, Thou hast made Thyself like to him in his human nature, not only as to his soul on which Thou didst impress Thine image, but as to his body,

* 1 St. John iv. 9. † St. John i. 14.

making Thyself flesh, and clothing Thyself with a body liable to suffering and death! Do, thou, then, O man, so loved, so honoured, so elevated by God, united in body and soul with the Divine Person, follow after not only eternal life and glory with thy whole soul, but in thy body also seek that real immortality and true life and glory which shall know no end.

CHAPTER X.

The love, which the Son of God shows to us in His Nativity, Circumcision, and Name of Jesus.

ALTHOUGH the Incarnation is the mystery that most fully shows forth to us the love of God for man, because, loving us with an infinite love, He has communicated to us that infinite good which is His own Divinity, and this in the most perfect way, in the union, that is, of human nature with the Divine Person; yet in the other mysteries wrought by Christ on earth He has in a high degree manifested the same love, since all include within them the benefit of the Incarnation, and add to it those other most especial and wonderful benefits which Christ in His love has bestowed upon us. Moreover, when showing in each mystery His immense love to us, Christ also manifests the love which His Eternal Father has for us. In the first place, because the love wherewith Christ as God loves us is, as we have shown, the very same love that God the Father bears towards us; and secondly, in everything which Christ did and suffered for man, from the moment of His Incarnation till He yielded His last breath upon the Cross, He was moved by the Eternal Father, Who wrought in Him all His interior and exterior actions, so that these are all effects and proofs of the love with which the Father has followed us.

And this same love of the Father for man, which Christ as man saw in Him, moved Him to each thing which of His own accord and of His own love He did for man. For at that very instant in which the Soul of Christ was created and joined to the Divine Person, It saw clearly the Divinity and was beatified in Its higher faculties. Thus seeing God, It saw in Him an immense love for man and that will according to which He desired that men should be loved and saved, as being more noble amongst His creatures, and from their fall through the fault of their progenitor lying exposed to eternal damnation; according to which He desired also that full restoration should be wrought out for them, and that He Himself should undertake this work, having it at heart, and giving full effect to it. When, therefore, the Soul of Christ, all inflamed with the fire of the Father's love, so greatly exalted by Him, and so filled with the desire of pleasing Him and of doing in everything His Divine will, saw the love that He, the Eternal Father, bore to man, and read His will that He Himself should love and save man, It was moved to love men as fully as It did, and to do and suffer for them all that It in very truth fulfilled.

So that all the works of Christ were not only effects and proofs of the love which His Soul, as human, bore to us, but gave testimony also of that immense love which He as God, along with His Eternal Father, had for us. And this was one of the chief objects of His coming into the world to declare to us this love of His Father, and to give the strongest testimony of it, in order to attract men's hearts and inflame them with the love of Him Who has so greatly loved them. Which He Himself intimated when He said: "*I am come to cast fire on the earth,*"*—the fire of love in the hearts of men, by telling the world of the love which My Father bears to it, teaching the same by word, and suffering and dying for it—"*and what will I but that it be kindled,* that men may burn with its flame.

* St. Luke xii. 49.

Among other mysteries of Christ's life, His holy Nativity shows Him to us born a little Infant of the Most Blessed Virgin, and subject to all the weakness and sufferings of other babes. Instead of coming as a man full grown, He willed to appear with a very small body, after having been carried nine months in the womb. Until born, infants have no consciousness of their existence, but Jesus ere yet brought forth had as perfect use of reason as He now enjoys in Heaven, whence His long concealment and long waiting was to Him full of humiliation and painful restraint. When born a very tender babe, He chose to suffer cold and all the other hardships of the season, the inconvenience of exposure and the roughness of the stable, He was wrapt in swaddling clothes, was suckled, and grew only gradually. Though full of wisdom, He passed His infancy like others in silence; and He subjected Himself to all these trials and humiliations that He might be more like to men and prove by these signs the greatness of His love, making Himself more amiable in the eyes of men, and inviting us more earnestly to His love. Hence St. Bernard: "God, mighty and to be greatly praised, is born a babe to be greatly loved." *

Christ also manifested His love to us in His Nativity by being laid in a manger. Because men had become through sin like to the brute animals, having, in their estrangement from spiritual and invisible things fixed their love and affection on those which are corporeal, and sought all their pleasure in them alone; they stood in need, therefore, of Divine and heavenly food to form a holy and spiritual life within them in exchange for their mere animal life, that from being men like the brute animals they might become spiritually minded. Christ then, as the Bread from Heaven and Food of eternal life, was born in a manger used for animals, that men feeding on Him with lively faith, acknowledging Him for their God and Saviour, and fixing their love and hope on Him, might

* *Serm. de Nat.*

be spiritually incorporated into Him and become one with Him, and might thus be changed from animals into spiritual and godlike men; converting, through the power of this Divine Infant given to them as food, their past sensual life into one pure and holy and worthy of being rewarded by that life which is blessed and everlasting.*

This same love Christ showed in the mystery of His Circumcision, wherein, when but eight days old, He desired to endure for us a pain which in the Divine Infant was most acute, from the peculiar delicacy and sensitiveness of a bodily frame more perfect than that of all other infants. Thus early did God will that by the sharp stone knife Blood should be drawn from His Most Sacred Body. And though the pain which He then felt and the Blood which He shed were the payment of most ample price for the redemption of man and his deliverance from the captivity of sin, as being of infinite value, yet He did not offer it as full payment and cancelling of the debt, but as part only. For, so great was the love through which He desired to save lost man, that He could not content Himself with giving an all-sufficient, He must give a superabundant price for it. Hence all that He ever suffered, whether in His Circumcision, or in the whole course of His life till He expired on the Cross, He offered as full payment and satisfaction for man's redemption.

Again, He has made manifest His love in the name of Jesus, which He then received. The name which God has expressly given to any of His servants has always indicated the quality or office conferred upon him. Thus when He gave to Abram the name of Abraham, He signified by this that Abraham should be the spiritual father of many faithful. In calling Simon, Cephas or Peter, He intimated that His Apostle was to be the firm foundation of His Church. In like manner, that the name of our Most Sacred Lord should be Jesus, and that this name should be given to Him from Heaven, signified that the office of this Infant was to

---

* See St. Cyril, *Luc.* ii. *in Caten.*

save men. Now the especial act of one who loves is to free him whom he loves out of evil and to confer good on him; and the more serious that evil is, and the more excellent the benefit conferred, the greater is the love which is exhibited. But no greater evil can exist than sin and the eternal damnation of body and soul, nor can benefit be greater than the salvation and spiritual life of the soul, the salvation and eternal life of both soul and body; yet from this evil does Jesus liberate us, and this benefit does He confer upon us, and herein lies His office. Therefore was He called Jesus, because, as the angel said, "*He shall save His people from their sins;*" * and saving them from these which slay and condemn them, He will justify them, giving them the life of grace and glory. And God by the mouth of Simeon declares that the salvation, which this Infant should work out, was not to be hidden, nor was He to effect it in a few men only, or in one nation only, but it was to be a salvation so public and manifest that He would work it out "*before the face of all peoples;*"† every one could share in it if he willed, of whatever nation or condition he might be.

Oh, how great and wonderful consolation to every son of man to whom, though lost and captive, such a Saviour has been given, bearing a name that so clearly and so surely tells His office to save all who desire to be saved through Him! Far keener is the solace and joy of one who experiences a benefit after some great evil, as health following on a long and grievous malady, or peace succeeding a state of violent excitement. How unspeakable, then, must have been the relief to man, who for five thousand ears from the beginning of the world lay exposed to the anger and enmity of God, the slave of sin and of the devil, sentenced to eternal death and damnation, when to him an Infant is given, gentle, kind, most sweet, most amiable; Who, though the Babe and Son of a Virgin, is, at the same time, the Son of the Most High God; Who comes bearing

* St. Luke ii. 31. † St. Matt. i. 21.

the title and office of the Saviour; and Who will truly free from sin all those that wish, and will secure to them victory over death and Hell, and entrance into Heaven.

Such are the works of love which that God hath wrought on the earth, as He Himself hath assured us. "*The Spirit of the Lord is upon Me,*" hath inspired and hath moved Me, as Man, to work out the salvation of the world, "*because that same Lord hath anointed Me,*" in perfect fulness, "*to preach His Gospel to the poor*" and those deprived of human help; "*He hath sent Me,*" that by this means they may become humble and meek to obey His Gospel; "*to heal the contrite of heart,*" those, namely, who are tempted by their evil passions and wounded by sin; "*to preach a release to the captives*" of Satan and the slaves of sin, "*and to them that are shut up deliverance*" and the freedom of grace. In other words, to those whose eyes are blinded by the darkness of error and wickedness I will restore light, for those whom corrupt morals and sinful practices have held bound I will burst the chains of their evil habits, and cause them to walk on sweetly in the way of the Divine law. "*And He hath sent Me to comfort all that mourn*" and are afflicted, that I might raise them up and strengthen them in their pity and compassion for the sins and sorrows of God's people. Such was the office which the Son of God came to fulfil upon the earth, and which is signified to us by His name of Saviour.*

---

* Isaias lxi. 1; St. Luke iv. 18.

CHAPTER XI.

Other proofs which Christ has given of His love for man, in calling all to His friendship and bestowing on them the Kingdom of Heaven.

ANOTHER testimony of Christ's exceeding great love for us was, that after leading a hidden life for thirty years, and passing forty days of rigid fasting in the wilderness, as soon as the fit age and time had come for manifesting Himself to Israel, He began to treat and converse most gently and familiarly with men, with the humble and simple-hearted, and even with such notorious sinners as were willing to be led on by His doctrine and example to do penance and correct their lives. Besides which, in order to show Himself most amiable to all, and most easy of imitation, in order to attract all to the path of life, and hold out to them the hope of healing and amendment, He took His food and meals with them in common, though observing the strictest temperance. He made use also of ordinary clothing and habitation, yet according to the most exact poverty.

By thus exercising virtues in the highest degree of perfection, He laid down an example for the guidance of all saints and of those who aspire after perfection. At the same time He conformed in some things to the ordinary life of man, marking out in the use of common things the true rule of virtue, and thus He showed the way of amendment to those weaker souls, who keeping to the level of common life, observe the commandments of God, yet dare not embrace the counsels of perfection, nor aspire after a higher degree. Thus in the breadth of His immense charity He included every kind and condition of men, of whatever rank or mode of life, if only they previously purposed to quit their sins and follow out the work of their salvation; and by this means, while He observed everything that was due to the Divinity of His Person and the dignity of His own most holy life, He yet condescended in every respect possible to the conditions of all, inclining their goodwill unto Himself, and leading them into the obedience and love of His Heavenly Father.

Another very clear testimony of His love was, that when the Eternal Father gave to Him, as Man, the dominion of everything, and full right of primogeniture over His goods, and made Him universal King of Heaven and earth (for in the very instant of His conception and of the creation of His most sacred soul, He was beatified and entered into His rule and dominion over all creatures), He would not stand alone in the possession of this power and glory, but willed to share it also with men whom He adopted as His brethren, and made them kings, and beatified, and of high degree in His Heavenly Court. That He might carry this out, in His first manifesting of Himself to Israel, He went on foot through all the towns and villages of Judea, preaching to all the Kingdom of Heaven, fully instructing them in its nature, stirring them up to desire it, and to dispose themselves rightly for attaining to it. In evidence of this the Evangelist wrote, "*The Lord travelled through the cities and towns, preaching and evangelizing the Kingdom of God*" to be given to men, "*and the twelve Apostles with Him.*"* And that they might remove sin, which deprived them of so great a good, they were directed to "*do penance, for the Kingdom of Heaven is at hand.*"† What was the kingdom thus announced to those dwelling upon earth? Clearly that which had come down from Heaven to earth. Who could offer to man this Kingdom of Heaven except the Son of God, Whose Kingdom that was, and Who held it in His hands to bestow on whomsoever He willed? And sending

---

* St. Luke viii. 1. † St. Matt. iii. 2.

out His disciples to preach, He bade them that they should do what He had done—that is, announce the Kingdom of Heaven as He had announced it, saying, "*The Kingdom of God is come nigh unto you.*"* That Kingdom which had been removed very far off and lost by the sin of the first man, and which hitherto neither Saint, nor Patriarch, nor Prophet had ever entered or seen, or given any clear idea of, was now made so near that the time had come for opening its gates, and every man who believed and did penance should enter into possession and enjoyment of it. And when our Lord stood before Pilate and bore testimony to the truth and nature of this Kingdom, He said, "*My Kingdom is not of this world.*"† It is not temporal, it is not earthly, like those of this world, that consist in possessing cities and wealth of but little value, and soon passing away, but it is a Heavenly Kingdom, giving possession of Heavenly goods and riches, both lasting and of immense value, and admitting into the enjoyment, through the beatific vision, of God Himself, and of the infinite and eternal good.

Oh, wondrous proof of the love of Christ our Lord for us is it that He should offer to us so great a Kingdom, and with such good will as to beg of us, and to account it a favour that we should dispose ourselves to receive it, and to derive great pleasure and glory to Himself that He should admit us into possession of it! Earthly kings are not wont to bestow their kingdoms on their favourites or servants, however dear to them, but only some particular lordship, or share of their rule; neither do they invite their subjects, however high in favour, to sit at their private table, but only, as a great act of courtesy, they send them some dish from their table. But Christ our Lord so loves His faithful servants as to give His own celestial Kingdom to them, to place them at His own Divine banquet, and to set before them some of the food which He Himself partakes of; nay, in yet more wonderful testimony of a still

---

* St. Luke x. 9. † St. John xviii. 36.

greater love, the very same portion of infinite sweetness, on which He Himself feeds, does He share with them, to wit, His own very Divinity, for He gives power to all to see, love, and enjoy His Divine essence. God indeed regards Himself with infinite perfection of vision, loves Himself with an infinite love, rejoices in Himself with an infinite joy; and this happiness and beatitude belongs only to God, is natural to Him, and is eternal. The Soul of Christ sees, loves, and enjoys the Divinity with the highest perfection and excellence which ever has been communicated, or can be communicated, to any creature; the Blessed also see and enjoy that same Divinity according to the degree of merit which each has attained. Although there must be this wide difference, yet all do certainly feed on and are nourished by one and the same food, all are enriched by the same good, all possess one and the same Kingdom of God, since all see, love, possess, and enjoy the Divinity of God.

And this love, wherewith Christ loves us, is like to that with which the Eternal Father loves Him, so that He told His disciples, "*As the Father hath loved Me, I also have loved you.*"* And He intimated the same when He thus addressed the Father: "*Father, I will that where I am*" according to My Divinity and the beatific vision of My Soul, "*they also whom Thou hast given Me,*" choosing them from eternity, and in time drawing them to faith and obedience in Me, "*may be with Me,*" and may clearly see with the eyes of their soul the glory of My Divinity, which Thou hast given and communicated to Me, uniting with it My Humanity in one and the same Divine Person.†

* St. John xv. 9. † St. John xvii. 24.

CHAPTER XII.

The signs of this love which Christ gave His disciples at the Last Supper, in washing their feet, and in instituting the Most Holy Sacrament of the Altar.

ALTHOUGH Christ did throughout the whole course of His life exhibit His exceeding great love for man, He gave still stronger proofs of it in the last night which He spent with His disciples. St. John says that Jesus, having in His most holy soul from the first moment of His conception loved exceedingly "*His own who were in the world*," and proved His love to them by words and works, never ceased to love them, "*He loved them unto the end*" of His life on earth, and then gave them the highest proofs of His love.* The first of these was when He saw how closely death was approaching Him, and at full leisure and with great solemnity sat at meat with His disciples. To eat at all with another is a mark of love. But when the near expectation of death weighs on the mind and fills it with bitterness, to keep at that moment all such oppression close shut within one's breast, retaining before others a calm and pleasant countenance, quietly to sit and eat in their midst with utmost composure, to cheer them with one's manner, to hand food to them, to give others with one's own hand portions from the dish, to allow another to lay his head upon one's own breast (as St. John was allowed), to converse sweetly and lovingly with all; such acts as these are indeed a wholly wonderful and most rare testimony of love.

Another evidence of this love was when, "*Knowing that the Father had given Him all things into His hands,*"†

* St. John xiii. 1.   † St. John xiii. 3.

with those very hands so full of power, He washed their feet defiled by sin, and wiped them with the cloth. For as God, infinite power over all things was in His eternal generation communicated to Him by the Father, and as man, He held supreme dominion over all creatures, with power of life and death, and all events, and at His disposal were placed salvation, redemption, grace, glory, and all else that the Father possessed. This humble act, then, He performed to men of such poor condition, neither out of impotence or weakness, nor yet, again, out of ignorance (for He knew that everything was subject to His will), but simply because His love for man was so boundless, that He judged nothing, however humble and despised, to be unbecoming a Lord of so great power and majesty, provided only it was necessary or conducive to the salvation, healing, or solace of men. As Theophylact wrote, "Since the Father has placed the salvation of the world in His hands, it was fitting that to Him also should be committed all that pertained to the salvation and spiritual good of souls."* And in a certain instruction of the Council of Ephesus it is said, "God not unjustly retains in His control all that which is the cause of salvation and of the healing of souls."

But the highest testimony of his love which Christ gave at the Last Supper was the institution of the most Holy Sacrament, wherein He left us His Sacred Body as food, and His most Precious Blood as drink. This action of His love was so profound a mystery that one, who by help of especial light from Heaven examined into the love which God therein showed, and penetrated the interior secrets of this mystery, reached at length so far into the immense abyss that for very amazement and admiration his intellect failed him, and his will was set on fire with flames of the most ardent affection, while his whole soul melted in the tenderest devotion of His love.† O sign, O testimony of love beyond all description, that He Whose

---

* *In Joan.* xiii.   † St. Thom. p. 3. q. 51. a. 1. ad 3.

infinite magnitude neither Heaven nor earth can contain, He who fills the Heaven of Heavens with His glory, and by His countenance beatifies all who dwell therein, He Who is adored by angels ministering before Him; that He, I say, should be willing to inclose Himself within the consecrated Host, and to be handled by man through the sacramental species, laid upon our tongues, pressed with our lips, and received within our bodies!—and thus hidden, that He should willingly visit our souls to heal our wounds, to cure our diseases, to strengthen our weaknesses, enlighten our ignorance, cheer our sadness, warm our tepidity into love, and satiate our hunger and thirst; that He should, yet more, give Himself for true food to man, and as each living man changes into himself the lifeless bread, imparting to it being and life, that He as the Living Bread of infinite efficacy should change man into Himself, imparting to him spiritual being and Divine life, making him like to Himself, humble, gentle, kind-hearted, full of charity and mercy, greatly pleasing and acceptable to His eternal Father, a man become spiritual and heavenly through His life!

In the mystery of His Incarnation He assumed our human nature and united it with His Divinity in one and the same Person. But in this most holy sacrament He gives to us His Sacred Humanity received from us, His glorious Body and His blessed Soul, and beside this His own Divinity; and that union of persons and communication of goods so peculiar to true love, that also has Christ effected in most perfect manner. Thus, as food becomes corporally one thing with him who eats it, so He, by the strictest union of faith and love becomes spiritually one thing with him who receives Him; and as food is all absorbed by him who takes it, so Christ communicates the whole of what He is, Body, Soul, and Divinity, together with all His gifts and merits, to the man who receives Him with purity of heart. Nor is this sacrament given to all men as common benefit, but it is a particular benefit given to each one. The Passion and death of Christ are general for all, and Christ liberally offers their fruit and efficacy to man in general, nor can any one man say this whole Passion and Death were for me alone. But the benefit of the most holy Sacrament is common to all, so as to be none the less particular to each one. In each consecrated Host Christ is wholly given to the receiver, enabling him to say, "Christ our Lord, contained within this Host which I receive, is wholly given and communicated to me." Hence in this most sublime mystery and benefit shines forth with especial clearness the immense love which Christ bears towards every just man, according to the hymn of the Church. The Lord's Body is given to His disciples, as wholly to each of them as it is wholly to all. On that first occasion He was given to them liable to suffering and death, as He then was; but since that He is given immortal, crowned with highest glory and ineffable sweetness, as He now is in Heaven.

CHAPTER XIII.

Of Christ's union, through the Blessed Sacrament, with the soul, and the fresh proof which this gives to us of His love.

SINCE the closer the union the greater the proof therein of love, we should consider that Christ, in the Most Holy Sacrament, unites Himself to us, not only by the spiritual union of grace and love, as in the other sacraments, but by a union which is, in a certain manner, real and corporal, and effects a more intimate and special spiritual union of grace and love than in the other sacraments. It is not that our Lord's Body quits the sacramental species to unite Itself with our body, nor is it that, remaining within the species, It spreads Itself through our bodies, and unites

Itself with all their parts; but the Body of Christ unites Itself to our bodies through the sacramental species, in that part where these remain, and the union continues during the whole time that the species last. On the one hand, this union ordinarily produces spiritual effects in the soul of him who receives, by removing venial sins when it finds him otherwise well disposed, by increasing grace, purity, and all infused virtues, by stirring the heart to devotion and present fervour, by imparting spiritual joy, and by communicating actual helps for overcoming temptations, and for performing holy and difficult works; and on the other hand, it produces most admirable effects in the body, mitigating and regulating the passions of anger, impurity, gluttony, together with those others situated in the sensitive appetite, and causing in their stead great peace, calm of mind, and consolation. These effects it produces, not only by the increase of grace and virtue, but also by supplying holy affections and desires, and by communicating those particular aids which promote this end.

The Blessed Sacrament, in addition, imparts to the bodies of the just the glory of the universal resurrection in which they are to share, whence Holy Communion is the germ and pledge of the immortality and eternal glory of the body, and the Council of Nice calls this most Divine Sacrament "a sign of the resurrection." St. Ignatius says it is "the medicine of immortality."* St. Cyril that it is "the food which nourishes immortal bodies, giving them life and eternal glory."† This it effects in the bodies of the just, not through that general grace common to all the sacraments, to which the glory both of soul and body is allied, but through means peculiar to this Sacrament, through special helps and aids particularly directed to the overcoming of temptations, and to perseverance in a holy life until death. It implants also in the bodies of just men an especial title, principle of life, and right, in favour of which they attain to eternal glory, insomuch as they are

* Epist. xiv. *ad Ephes.*   † Lib. iv. *in S. Joan.* cap. xvi.

united through it to the glorious Body of Christ, and thus more largely participate in the virtue that proceeds from It, and are made more worthy of a glorious immortality.

This union is named by the saints a natural union, a corporal union of the Body of Christ with our own, a mingling of His flesh with ours, a conversion of our flesh into that of Christ.* In conformity with these words, we receive the natural Body of Jesus Christ neither in figure, nor vaguely, nor solely by faith and love, through simply believing in and loving Him, but we receive Him in very truth. And from this corporal receiving of Christ, this true union and contact in some measure with His Sacred Body, springs spiritual union between Christ and our souls through faith, love, and charity, and from that again spring certain spiritual effects which Christ works in our bodies, and which conduce to this spiritual union. Since the union thus effected is more perfect, and our soul partakes more largely of Christ, and enjoys fuller communication with His soul, and since the just man becomes more distinctly in soul and body a possession and a living member of Christ, Who therefore takes a particular care of him; so a worthy Communion gives a new and especial title to fuller participation in Christ's power and in the abundance of His gifts and spiritual graces. In this way the Blessed Sacrament is beyond all description the fullest testimony of His love. And with so great liberality and readiness does Christ give us all the precious fruits of this Sacrament, that He leaves this infinite treasure at our disposal to make it our own as often as we wish, and He invites and begs us to apply for it repeatedly.

Again, this infinite good is not offered us during a limited time only, but for our whole lives, even till the end of the world. Rich properties are often left by fathers to their sons that they may hold them during life; but their sons perhaps soon dissipate and waste the whole. It is not thus with that infinite good, that everlasting inheritance

* Hilar. lib. viii. *de Trinitate;* Cyril lib. x. *in S. Joan.* cap. xiii.

which the infinite power and goodness of God preserves for us; no man can exhaust it by his sins, or fritter it all away by his abuse of it; it ever remains safe and intact for the sinner to enjoy again as often as he returns and repents. Nor do those only enjoy its possession who have always been holy, and have always received this most Blessed Sacrament worthily, but those also who have been sinners, and have made bad Communions, if only after confession they approach with earnest penitence, can begin to draw abundant fruit from it. A still further sign of Christ's love we have in this, that He is always, through this Blessed Sacrament, present in the midst of us, not only as to His Divinity, which is everywhere, but also as to His sacred Humanity, which is both in Heaven at the right hand of His Father, and likewise in the Sacrament of the Altar. He does not dwell there in visible form, but hidden beneath the Sacramental species, that we may gain fresh merit by believing in a mystery invisible to carnal eyes, and by desiring and loving our Lord, Whom we hope to see clearly in the courts above. Hence, while dwelling in our midst upon the altar, He is ever renewing our memory of Him, and deepening our thoughts, our desires, and our love towards Him. To perpetuate amongst us His Divine presence in the sanctuary and His sacramental life, He granted to His disciples and through them to all priests the power of constantly renewing that great mystery. "*Do this for a commemoration of Me.*" By this He made them priests, and gave them authority over His true body united to the Divinity, that as often as they willed, while still the world endured, they might again consecrate it. By impressing on their souls a character or spiritual mark which can never be effaced, He confirmed still more the authority that He had before given them over His mystical body, the Church, when He said, "*Whatsoever you shall bind upon earth shall be bound also in Heaven, and whatsoever you shall loose upon earth shall be loosed also in Heaven.*"* The bestowal of both offices

---

* St. Matt. xviii. 18.

completed their sacerdotal character, giving them power to consecrate His Body, and to bind or loose souls from sin, making them dispensers of His Heavenly riches, ministers of the Divine sacraments, judges and teachers of the world. To men mortal and weak in themselves He granted a share of His rule over Heaven and earth, the keys of eternal life and death, and spiritual authority to direct kings and men of influence in the world. And all this proceeded from the great love of Christ for men, and was appointed in order to inflame their hearts with true love towards their Creator and their Saviour.

CHAPTER XIV.

The love which Christ manifested in His sermon after the Last Supper.

CHRIST gave another very clear indication of His love for His disciples and for all the elect in His discourse at the Last Supper, narrated by St. John in five successive chapters. His words then were so many bright rays of love and flames of burning charity, disclosing wondrous mysteries and secrets of the future. He proved, as He Himself told them, the strength of His love by intrusting these secrets to them, "*I have called you friends: because all things whatsoever I have heard of My Father*," which it behoves you to know, "*I have made known to you.*"[*] With great earnestness, and in many words, He exhorted them to love one another, thus manifesting the intense ardour of His own love for all; for he who with a deep and pure affection loves a friend does his best to make others love him. He forewarned His disciples also of the labours, persecutions, and afflictions that awaited them, and encouraged them to the patient endurance of these.

* St. John xv. 15.

He consoled them by announcing the great glory which would be theirs, as that future reward wherein they might hope to be like their Master, when all their sadness would be changed into never-fading joy. He addressed them by the tender names of "disciples," "friends," "children," and plainly confessed to them that He loved them greatly, and that His Father also loved them. "*As the Father hath loved Me I also have loved you; and the Father Himself loveth you, because you have loved Me.*"*
He promised that He would never desert them, would not leave them orphans, but would visit, console, strengthen, accompany, and dwell always with them, both by the true omnipresence of His Divinity ruling, preserving, and operating in all things, and by the hidden presence of His sacred Humanity in the Sacrament of the Altar, and by the constant assistance of His grace.

He specially promised them the coming of the Holy Ghost, the Comforter, and the fulness of Divine gifts which this coming should communicate to them. He announced the peace and spiritual joy which they were to cherish in their souls, whatever dangers surrounded them, as well as the admirable fruit they should bring forth in the world; in fine, that weight of heavenly glory that He will bestow on them, placing them at the supper-table of His Divine Presence in the Heavenly Kingdom. He prayed to His Eternal Father for them, beseeching Him to keep them safe, to deliver them out of all evil, to sanctify them, to bind them together in the most perfect union of mutual charity, to raise them to be with Christ in Heaven, that they might clearly see the infinite beauty of His Divine glory, and might be blessed, as He then was, in His Soul, and would be in His Body after He had arisen in the glory of His Immortality. We cannot gather the full meaning of Christ's words and promises in this sublime discourse, without learning much of that immense love wherewith His Heart was all on fire. In this we

---

* St. John xv. 9; xvi. 27.

are further helped by considering the time when they were uttered, for it was on that same night and on the day following that the sufferings of His Passion and death were about to exceed all that He had ever yet endured, or would endure, in time to come. On the day when one is awaiting the avenging stroke of death ready to fall upon him, he has no thoughts to spare for friends and kindred, but is altogether absorbed in the thought of the penalty hanging over him, and in seeking some relief and solace for his distress; nor does his anxiety of mind allow him to attend to anything else. But Christ, on that night when the fiercest passions of the world and of hell were raging round Him, and He saw them thirsting to take His life with the most frightful tortures, seemed forgetful of all that He had to endure, and with calm and serene mind, with a sweet and benign countenance, unmarked by sign of fear, He strengthened His disciples with so prolonged and mysterious a discourse; He enlightened, encouraged, and confirmed them, and with heavenly promises rejoiced their soul. Such proof of fortitude and constancy was worthy of a Man Who was by nature the begotten Son of God, worthy also of that most ardent love wherewith He loved the sons of Adam, and of His own accord gave Himself up to suffer and die for their salvation.

CHAPTER XV.

Of the love which Christ manifested in His Passion, and which He signified in the thirst, caused by His desire to save us and to suffer for us.

To endure sufferings in behalf of a person beloved is a great proof of love. And the more severe these are, and the stronger the desire to endure them, so much the greater is the proof of love which they afford. Christ had a vehement desire that the hour of His death should approach, and this out of His strong desire to suffer. When the time had come He was full of joy, as His own words bear witness: "*With desire I have desired to eat this pasch with you.*"* He desired this occasion of eating the paschal lamb, because it was to put an end to all the sacraments and sacrifices of the Old Law by the institution of new sacraments, and because, as St. Chrysostom wrote,† He was to enter immediately on His Passion and death, in order to save a perishing world. This intense desire He manifested by passing at once from the Last Supper to the Garden, where He knew His enemies would come to seize Him. He manifested it a second time by leaving the Garden as soon as He has finished the prayer to His Father, and meeting His enemies and presenting Himself to them, with the words: "*I am He.*" Though they carried lanterns and His Person was well known to them, and to Judas in particular, yet they did not recognize Him, for He was unwilling that they should until He had given Himself up to them, and had restored to them the power of knowing Him. At the same time He made it evident that, although He could by His infinite power have destroyed them, for by a single word He had driven them backward, falling helpless on the ground, yet He willed not to defend Himself, but restored their liberty of action to them, so that they could lay hold of Him and inflict on Him whatever cruelties and indignities they pleased. Thus did He show His great desire of suffering, and the immense love that moved Him to it.

The same did He testify when, with so great ignominy, He was hurried, with His hands bound, through the streets and lanes of Jerusalem, and made to stand before the several tribunals of Annas, Caiaphas, Pilate, and Herod, being subjected to such pain and disgrace in the presence of each judge, to blows, strokes, rebuffs, thorns, scourging,

* St. Luke xxii. 15. † *Hom. in S. Matt.* cap. xxvi.

filthy spittle, striking with the reed, injury to His flesh, trampling under foot, the veiling of His face, and plucking out of His hair, amid taunts and mockery; all which He bore as if He had been a malefactor, and deserving only reproof and infamy. At the same time that these torments and insults were beyond all count, each individual one was a most wondrous testimony of love, seeing that He Who suffered it was the Lord of infinite majesty, worthy of infinite glory, and that each was inflicted by vile and wicked men, and was submitted to for the sake of sinners and of enemies utterly undeserving of any benefit.

Especially was the love of Christ exhibited in His death on the Cross, inasmuch as it was the most terrible and disgraceful of all the sufferings heaped on Him; and in the manner in which He was fastened to the Cross, with arms distended, limbs violently drawn asunder, and His Body covered with blood, He proved how fully He had, out of love, given up everything He possessed and Himself also, that He might embrace us in the arms of His love. He died with His sacred flesh torn open by the thongs of the scourges, and His Heart pierced through by the lance, for a token that He would fain hide us within His Wounds and shelter us in His Heart. But it was when He exclaimed, "*I thirst*," that He in a more marked way expressed His love. For though His corporal thirst must have been excessive and hard for Him to bear, while He would have refused to assuage it with water, and knew in truth that no one would have brought it to Him; yet what He spoke of then was the far more torturing thirst of His anxious longing for our salvation. He earnestly desired our sanctification, our salvation, our glory; He longed to join us to Himself in the most perfect union of love and of the beatific vision. As the thirsty man drinks water with eager satisfaction, receives it into his body, and incorporates it with himself, so He thirsted after us as some restoring cordial, that He might closely unite us to His Sacred Heart, and make us one with Himself in highest spiritual gratification and delight.

Such was the desire that from the fire of love raging within His Heart burst forth in the cry, "*I thirst.*" The torments which He had hitherto endured reached in His Sacred Body the full height of suffering possible with life, yet all were surpassed by the love with which He bore them, and which therefore urged Him on to suffer still more, that He might give yet fuller testimony to the value He set on man's redemption, and to the boundless extent of His love towards those for whom He suffered. To use the words of the devout Tauler, it is as though He said, "Behold Me, O man, thus exhausted and consumed for the sake of thy salvation. See what horrible pains and griefs I undergo. Not yet is My Heart satisfied, far is My desire from being fully reached, and the flame of My love is not extinguished. If it be possible for Me and pleasing to My Father, a thousand times would I again be crucified to save each one, or would even hang in the midst of these sorrows until the Last Day of the Great Judgment. All this would I do most gladly if only I could make thee clearly see the immensity of the love of My Heart for thee, could soften thy stony heart, and kindle in thee the flame of obedience and love to My Heavenly Father."*

CHAPTER XVI.

Of the Love of Christ in refusing all sensible consolation during His torments on the Cross.

CHRIST proved His love in the interior suffering of the highest part of His nature, which made Him cry aloud: "*My God, My God, why hast Thou forsaken Me?*" From the instant in which Christ was conceived, His most

* *De Passione,* cap. xlvii.

holy soul looked upon the Divine essence, was supremely blessed, and enjoyed the highest felicity; and since, according to the ordinary law, it is granted to the body that the beatitude of the soul should be communicated by way of redundance to it, in virtue of their mutual union, Christ caused that in some wonderful manner the glory flooding all His being should be restrained as though held captive within the superior functions of His Soul, nor spread from them to His Body and to His inferior faculties; and this He did that He might be able to suffer and to die for man. Nor did He only prevent that communication of glory from the superior to the inferior part of His being, which takes place in the glorified bodies of the Blessed, but during the season of His Passion He also withheld from the inferior part all the consolation and sensible joy granted to the saints and to many martyrs, who, even before their beatification, received into the sensitive part of their nature such strength and support from the spiritual graces of their souls, that they felt their sufferings far less keenly, and were sometimes enabled even to rejoice and exult in the midst of the pains and torments which they underwent. But Christ did not allow the same in Himself. He suspended all this consolation and joy, in order to make His torments more grievous to Him, and their every pang more sharp and penetrating; hence His cry: "*My God, My God, why hast Thou forsaken Me?*" God had not forsaken Him as regards the union with His Divinity, to which, in the Divine Person of Christ, His human nature must ever remain united; neither had God forsaken Him as regards His love, and the care which He took of Him, seeing that He must ever love Him as His true natural Son, and ever look on Him with the eyes of a Father, Who was perfectly well pleased in Him; but He had forsaken Christ as regards His Body and the inferior operations of His Soul, allowing Him to lie in a state of pure suffering, without the slightest alleviation or sensible comfort.

Christ did not utter these words as though complaining of this dereliction; indeed, we see that He Himself wished and preferred it. He uttered them that He might make known the full reality of His Passion and torments, the greatness of His sufferings, and His deprivation of all support or consolation in them. Whence this dereliction was the bitterest of all His pains, for had He not been thus forsaken by His Father, all His other sufferings would have been far lighter and easier to bear, but this had deepened immeasurably the pang of each one to him. He willed that this bitterness should add its weight to each torment He underwent, in order that the vilest of sinners, the sons of wrath, exposed to eternal damnation, might obtain pardon and sanctification, that they might become the sons of God, and attain to everlasting happiness; and in order that the absolution and satisfaction for their sins, obtained through His merits, should be the more complete and abundant, not only by reason of the quality of the Person Who suffered, but in consideration of the extent and intensity of that which He suffered, and this was a testimony of unspeakable value to the immense love which Christ bore towards the children of men.

When God descended on Mount Sinai to deliver the law to men, the mount was surrounded by terrible flames, "*which burned even unto Heaven*," * representing the glory of the Lord Who spoke to Moses. The true counterpart of this figure was the mystery of Mount Calvary, where Christ, seated on the chair of the Cross, by His own act and by His example taught men what they must do to save their souls. He thence promulgated to them the law and good pleasure of God which they must obey if they would gain Heaven, namely, that they should embrace the Cross, and follow in His footsteps, dying in all things to sin, and crucifying their own wills that they might obey the will of God. The love of Christ

---

* Deut. iv. 11.

was made manifest on Calvary that it might fill the whole world, and from Heaven might spread over all the earth, gathering within it every creature, and pouring forth its benefits everywhere. The glory of the Lord was manifested in its flames, showing forth most perfectly the infinite goodness of God, which is His glory, for it is on account of this one above all His other perfections that He is loved and glorified. His perfections of power, wisdom, and justice were made clearly known to man in the creation and government of the world, and in the terrible punishments of sinners, but His goodness had not before this been so manifest—it had delayed to shine forth till it burst out brightly from Mount Calvary in all that fire of love wherein Christ suffered and died for men. Wherefore our Lord said, "*I, if I be lifted up from the earth, will draw all things to Myself.*"* By suffering and dying on the Cross, He would satisfy for sin and redeem a lost world; and by manifesting on the Cross the greatness of His love towards men, He would inflame their hearts with love, and unite them unto Himself in love and obedience to His most holy law.

CHAPTER XVII.

On the love manifested by Christ after His Resurrection, in the wounds on His Sacred Body, and in His appearances when risen from the dead.

IT was fitting that Christ, after manifesting in His life and death the greatness of His love for man, should again manifest the same when risen from the dead, in proof of the continuance of that love, now that He is crowned with the glory of His Immortality at the right hand of His Father, and is acknowledged and worshipped

* St. John xii. 32.

on earth as truly God. The witnesses of His love were, in the first place, the marks of His Passion, which He willed to retain in His glorified Body—not as fresh wounds, but as being incorruptible and most glorious, full of splendour and Divine sweetness, adorned with the most perfect beauty, destined to testify and proclaim to all eternity the great things which Christ endured for man.* Were a soldier to receive some terrible wound when warding off from his king a blow aimed against his life, he would particularly desire that the scar should remain, and be observed by all, so high a gratification and glory would he esteem it to have been wounded in such a cause. In like manner, our Lord retained the scars of the chief wounds which He had received in His feet, hands, and side, in order to show the great gratification and pleasure He drew from His sufferings, and His desire that these sufferings should be known to all.

Another motive with Him was that he might exhibit these glorious marks to His heavenly Father, pleading their merits as our Advocate before Him, and thus drawing Him in His goodness and mercy to love us for the sake of His Son, to apply to us the fruit of His Passion, and to communicate to us, on account of His sufferings, His gifts and graces, and the reward of His glory. He felt too that we, in this our land of exile, could have no fear of His forgetting us, so long as He preserved ever before His own eyes the pledges which He had Himself given of His love.

As further testimony that He preserved this same love after His Resurrection, He appeared on the very day that He rose again to those holy women who were so afflicted and overwhelmed with fear, whom by His most gracious presence and sweetest words He consoled and encouraged, and filled with wonderful joy, saying to them, "*All hail, fear not.*"† To prove the same love, He joined Himself to the disciples going to Emmaus. These,

---

* St. John xx. 27.   † St. Matt. xxviii. 9.

besides being of the inferior degree of the seventy-two disciples, doubted also in their belief, and had grown cold in charity, yet He, the mighty Lord, Whom all angels serve and adore, under the appearance of a stranger follows upon their steps, and converses all the way with them, removing their sadness, enlightening their ignorance, strengthening them, and inflaming them with His love, as though these men, so humble, had been His equals. Another proof of His love He gave on the same day to the ten Apostles, whom He visited in their closed chamber, and appeared suddenly in their midst, so as to be seen by all, that He might, like a sun amongst the stars, illuminate them with His Divine presence, like a general at the head of his soldiers animate them by His prowess, like the heart in the midst of the members, send forth new life into them, or, like a friend fill them with joy and comfort. So, standing amongst them all, He again and again saluted them, saying, "*Peace be to you.*"* And by this word He intimated to them the love which the eternal Father bore to them for His sake, since through the merits of the Passion of the Son they were now united in peace with Him, and fully reconciled; as also He by it announced that reconciling love of peace and union which He desired that they, as true sons and His most dear brethren, should ever preserve amongst themselves, and that most resplendent and never-ending peace of the glory which His merits had obtained for them.

Similar was the manifestation of His love to the seven disciples whilst fishing in the Sea of Tiberias. For, standing on the shore without revealing Himself, He with affectionate interest inquired: "*Children have you any meat?*"† meaning fish so dressed as to be eaten with bread. And on their replying that, although labouring all the night, they had caught nothing, He desired at once to recompense their toil and take refreshment with them. He bade them let down their nets on the right side of the

* St. John xx. 19.   † St. John xxi. 5.

boat, and by granting them a miraculous draught He opened their eyes to recognize Him. He next prepared instantaneously a meal for them, by the ministry of an angel He lighted a fire on the shore, cooked a large fish, and placing bread beside it, invited His disciples to partake. And this He did, from no need of food in which He Himself stood, being the most High God, but simply for their comfort and for the clearer manifestation of the truth of His Resurrection. Thus the King of Glory, already entered on its eternal possession, made these poor fishermen eat of this fish and this bread, Himself served it to them, and ate along with them.

After this, "*He opened their understanding that they might understand the Scriptures.*"* It was thus especially that He gave to these rude and illiterate fishermen wisdom and light from Heaven, enabling them to penetrate Divine mysteries and to become teachers of the world. Such was the beginning of His converse with them during the forty days after His Resurrection, in which He frequently spoke to them of the Kingdom of God, described to them the future condition of the Church Militant, and those immense rewards they should hereafter enjoy in the Church Triumphant, and instructed them in all the virtues necessary for securing the possession of that Heavenly felicity. By visible signs and proofs did He illuminate their minds in the true faith, by the most precious gifts and the sweetest endearments did He inflame their hearts with charity and love to God, while He also filled their souls with the sure hope of His Heavenly Kingdom by the liberal promises and the earnest of interior graces and consolations which He gave them.

Yet one other testimony of love Christ vouchsafed in His appearance on the mountain in Galilee to the eleven Apostles, along with the seventy-two disciples, and five hundred of the brethren at once.† This manifestation He had specially promised beforehand, both by His own mouth

---

* St. Luke xxiv. 45.   † 1 Cor. xv. 6.

and by the word of His angel, publishing it widely, naming the place, and designating the particular mountain. And to that whole assembly He announced that the Father had given all power to Him as Man in Heaven and in earth, and He directed His Apostles that they should go forth into the whole world to preach His Gospel and spread the fruits of His Passion amongst all nations, declaring to them His most holy will, in order that all might lay hold of His salvation of grace and eternal glory. Then He concluded by promising that He would be "*with them all days, even to the consummation of the world.*"*

By these and many other proofs Christ testified His great love to us in His Life, in His Death, in His Resurrection, how as Man, and still more as God, He loves us. For His most Sacred Humanity, and all that He did and suffered therein, is a living image of His Divinity, and is as a bright mirror in which we behold the infinite goodness, mercy, and love with which God embraces all the children of men.

CHAPTER XVIII.

On the means by which Christ taught us the nature of the love which we should bear towards God, and on that which constitutes the love of friendship.

CHRIST manifested His own love towards us not only for the purpose of stirring us up to love God, Who has so greatly loved us, but also of teaching us in what particular way we ought to love God. There is a certain love of God above all things, which is called love of esteem or appreciation,† and consists in this, that the faithful member of the Church values the observance of the Divine precept, and

---

* St. Matt. xxviii. 18, 20.
† St. Thomas 1. 2. q. 100, a. 10.

the execution of the Divine will, more highly than all created things, or his own very life, so that in a single act of his will he decides to give up everything he has or can have rather than violate God's precept or act against His will. Of this love the lowest degree is, as we have before stated, when the Christian so places before everything the observance of a Divine command binding under sin, as to resolve not to consent to mortal sin for the sake of any created thing, and to sacrifice everything rather than commit it. But the highest grade of this love is that which so places the observance of every Divine precept and the execution of the Divine will before all created things, and before life itself, as to carry out with the utmost care and labour possible everything which it understands that God wishes, and rather than thwart or be guilty of the slightest fault against it, to sacrifice willingly everything that it can lose in this world. This constitutes *appreciative* love, and it admits of this latitude of degree in the question of estimation, though there are other degrees of more or less intensity in love, of which, however, we do not here speak. But it is this that we call the *love of friendship for God*, for it is a characteristic peculiar to true and perfect friends that they should share in the same desires and dislikes, so that what the one wishes the other wishes also, and what the one rejects the other rejects also. Now, to make our friendship with God true and perfect there must be between God and man but one liking and one disliking, and since it is evident that God should not be subject to the will of man, who is His creature, and whose will is prone to error, it follows that man should be subject in all things to the will of God, Who is his Creator, and Whose will is rectitude itself, the rule and measure of all virtues.

This obligation under which man lies of in everything doing the will of God, if he is to preserve His friendship, Christ intimated to His disciples when He said, " *You are My friends*," cherishing true and perfect friendship with Me, and I with you, " *if you do the things which I command you.*"* The commandments of God declare what His will is, and the keeping of each of these secures the fulfilment of His will in all necessary things. For an act of love which really places the Divine precept above every created thing, and which is resolved to abandon everything else in order to keep it, embraces within itself, as in the root and cause, the fulfilment of all the commandments of God, and from this resolve and determination, as from a principle and source, proceeds a full and perfect obedience to the Divine law. Hence we say that the man who possesses this love carries out every precept, because he cannot continue to possess this love without obeying God in the manner we have just indicated. According to this are the words of Christ, "*He that hath My commandments and keepeth them, he it is that loveth Me. And if any man love Me he will keep My word.*"† Such is the strength and virtue of *appreciative* love, when it is perfect, that it destroys all mortal sin that stands in the way of keeping God's commands, and admits no sin opposed to the Divine law. Wherefore it is compared to fire, a strong fire bright in flames, and fire permits no admixture of any contrary power without doing its best to destroy it. The earth, however dry, admits moisture; water, though cold, receives heat; the air, when warm and moist, can become both cold and clear. Fire alone, of its own nature hot and dry, rejects both cold and wet, and wherever it encounters them acts with full effect against them, till it consumes and destroys them. In like manner, the love of God, if imperfect, rejects at least mortal sin, but if perfect, allows, as far as it can, no sin whatever, but contends against and destroys it. Thus St. Augustine,‡ "The perfection of charity is the absence of all strong desire," that is, of all inordinate love, and so of all guilt. Divine love, too, is called in Scripture "*as strong as death,*"§ inasmuch as it makes men die to vice and sin, destroying them all, that God may live, and

---

* St. John xv. 14.   † St. John xiv. 21, 23.
‡ Tom. iv. L 83, q. 36, c. viii.   § Cant. viii. 6.

His will be perfectly obeyed. This *appreciative* love is the principal and most perfect love of God, since what God especially desires and is most rejoiced to see in man is the due estimation of His commandments and their fulfilment out of love, and full conformity and union with His will springing from the same love. This love is the test and touchstone of all other acts and exercises of the love of God, for if they hate and uproot all sin and offence done to God, and are directed to the most exact execution of His will, they are acknowledged to be true and solid acts of love ; but if notably deficient in these, they are not acts of true love of God. " *He who saith that he loveth God*," with the knowledge of a living faith, " *and keepeth not His commandments is a liar*," because both in word and act he asserts a falsehood, and therefore as to this point " *the truth is not in him*."*

CHAPTER XIX.

Examples, by help of which Christ has taught us this love.

CHRIST has by deeds and by words taught us how to practise this love. In everything which, from the instant of His conception until the moment of His death He either did, said, or thought as Man, He performed the will of His Eternal Father with the utmost possible perfection. So careful was He as to this point and with so great diligence did He carry it out, that He asserted it was for this very purpose that He descended from Heaven and was born into this world. " *I came from Heaven*," and humbled Myself to become Man, " *not to do My own*" human " *will, but the will of Him*," My Father, " *that sent Me ;*"† that as, according to the Divine Nature, we are but of one will, so My will, according to

* 1 St. John ii. 4. † St. John vi. 38.

My Human Nature, should be conformed in everything to His will, and that I should in all respects obey Him. For this reason I will, not only whatever He wills, but simply because He wills it. In this He said that He directed His whole life in the most faithful execution of all that the Father enjoined Him. "*I must work the works of Him that sent Him, while it is day;*"* or in other words: It is my duty, as Man, to do all those works which My Father hath enjoined on Me, all the miracles and wonders, all the acts of charity, humility, patience, and whatever else it becomes Me to do for the salvation of souls, for these are the works of the Father and are done by His power, good pleasure, and appointment. And in this I shall occupy Myself, while the day of My life and of My corporal and visible presence upon earth endureth.

All this Christ fulfilled with so great readiness and delight, that He accounted it His sweetest and most nourishing food, as He Himself told His disciples: "*My meat is to do the will of Him that sent Me, that I may perfect His work,*" the salvation of man.† As though He had said: Men desire greatly and think much of food, as sustaining their lives and affording them no little gratification; but that which I earnestly desire and highly esteem and especially relish is that I may do the will of My Father and obey His commands.

Our Lord also teaches us that the execution of the will and observance of the precepts of God are to be preferred to all those things which man loves and values in this life, and that all such are to be sacrificed in order that the will of God be done. To enforce this lesson, at the age of twelve years He left the company of His most dearly-beloved Mother and of St. Joseph, and "*remained behind in the Temple,*"‡ without having either forewarned them or asked their permission. Yet He had been most

---

* St. John ix. 4.
† St. John iv. 34.   ‡ St. Luke ii. 41.

anxious to please His Blessed Mother and to avoid causing her any pain or grief. He had with equal care consoled and obeyed St. Joseph, whom He esteemed as a father. But now, in order to fulfil His Eternal Father's will, He knowingly and without taking any leave of them stayed in the Temple, denied this pleasure to our Lady and St. Joseph, and decided on causing them very great pain.

On another occasion, while our Lord was addressing a large number in a certain house, the most holy Virgin, along with some of His relations, approached Him, and not being able to enter in, stopped for some time at the door. When a bystander remarked: "*Behold Thy Mother and Thy brethren stand without, seeking Thee*," our Lord did not interrupt His own discourse to answer him; but, on concluding it, He stretched out His hands towards His disciples saying: "*Behold My Mother and My brethren; for whosoever shall do the will of My Father that is in Heaven, he is My brother, and sister, and mother*."* He then went forth to comfort the Blessed Virgin and His relations with His most gracious presence. According to His natural inclination, our Lord would gladly have joined those waiting for Him; but, knowing it to be the will of His Father that He should finish His address begun and administer the Divine food to souls, He denied this consolation to those whom He loved, in order to accomplish the will of His Father and place His Father's good pleasure above all creatures.

Christ still further instructed us by word, as well as by example, that in the fulfilment of our duty of love every kind of suffering and calamity should be undergone, and every beloved object be given up, even life itself. When, after the Last Supper, He was addressing His disciples, and the time had come in which, according to the will of His Eternal Father, He should lead the way into the garden and there meet His enemies and deliver Himself

---

* St. Matt. xii. 46, 50.

up to death, however terrible and opposed to nature the act was, He at once set about accomplishing it and preparing for His death. This He also signified to His disciples : "*That the world may know that I love the Father, and as the Father hath given Me commandment, so do I. Arise, let us go hence,*"* to the place where I shall deliver Myself into their hands. After He was seized, St. Peter rashly struck the servant, thus seeking to defend our Lord by violence, but Christ indicating to him the will of His Father and the Divine command that He should give His life for the salvation of the world, and showing that He suffered most willingly and would have no hindrance placed in the way, said to Peter : "*Put up thy sword into the scabbard. The chalice which My Father hath given Me, shall I not drink it?*"† by which He meant, It is the will and appointment of My Father that I should suffer and die, therefore I desire that no impediment may be put to my Passion by any one, for the very reason that My Father hath so ordained it, it is fitting that I desire the same, love it, and hold it most welcome, even as refreshing drink is grateful to the thirsty man.

By such examples in His Life and Passion He taught us how to exercise this love which prefers the Divine will to everything, and how to deny with a willing mind our own inclinations, as well as our own will and that of all other creatures, and to offer ourselves for the endurance of any pain or trial in the fulfilment of God's will. He showed likewise how much He wished us to imitate Him in doing this, promising that he would, in reward, love us with all the affection of His most Sacred Heart, and would bestow on us all those gifts of grace and glory which He reserves in full measure for those who are especially dear to Him. As He has said, "*If you keep My commandments, you shall abide in My love,*" being most constantly beloved by Me. And it is but just that

* St. John xiv. 31.   † St. John xviii. 11.

you should keep them, "*as I also have kept My Father's commandments,*" obeying in all things His will, and so do abide in His love."*

CHAPTER XX.

How we are to exercise the love of complacency and benevolence towards God. Examples of this love given us by our Lord.

AFTER describing and giving examples of appreciative love of *friendship* and *obedience*, we come to another division of this virtue, which is called the love of *complacency*, and springs from the habit itself of charity. This love is shown by the faithful man, who from his heart takes delight in those good things which are in God, and which God possesses in the persons of creatures. He rejoices that God is that which He is, that He is one in nature and three in Persons, that He is infinite and eternal, dependent on none, infinitely powerful, wise, beautiful, good, and all perfect in blessedness; for these are the good things which are in God. He also takes delight in the knowledge that God is clearly seen by the Blessed in Heaven, is ever loved with the most perfect love, is praised and glorified by that most perfect and unceasing praise and glory that all are rendering Him for ever, and that on earth He is acknowledged by faith, adored, worshipped, loved, and honoured by all the just in purity of heart and sanctity of life; for these are the good things which God possesses in the persons of His creatures, since He gave these to them for their use and His own glory.

Out of this act and exercise of the love of complacency arises another, the love of *benevolence*, which desires the good of the person beloved; and since the just man who

* St. John xv. 10.

loves God draws great pleasure from the praise and glory offered up to God by the Blessed in Heaven, and by such as are just on earth, he longs that all other men, deprived as yet of so great a good, should come to know God by a true faith, should learn to love Him with their whole hearts, and to serve Him in purity of life, till they too are so blessed as to love and praise Him with all perfection in Heaven. But as God cannot increase that good which is in Himself, since He is infinite, and there is no other good that can be desired for Him than the external one of praise and glory from His creatures, it follows that to desire this is to bear towards Him the love of benevolence. If, however, this twofold love of complacency and benevolence be only exercised as it ought, it is most agreeable to God, and of great utility and merit to the soul, and, in the words of St. Bonaventure, " The soul finds therein a wonderful joy and most sweet delight, hence it is well that in its exercise the soul should exclaim : ' *It is good for us to be here.*' "*

But to know how it is to be fully exercised, we must observe that this love of complacency and benevolence can be imperfectly practised without grace or supernatural charity, since its acts are easy and attainable by the help of nature and of faith alone, and even where sin is, they can be wrought through that natural love by which the creature tends to the Creator. Wherefore he who would exercise this twofold love must necessarily have first practised the love of appreciation and obedience. For that appreciative love which prefers the execution of God's will to every other thing, and is determined to admit no sin, as being opposed to the Divine will, but would rather endure any suffering or calamity, cannot be obtained through the strength of nature alone, but requires the supernatural help of God, and when it is obtained, grace and charity necessarily accompany it. The reason of this is that in the pious Christian, who through faith acknowledges God to

* Tom. ii. in l. *Parvum bonum*, p. 2.

be, not only the Author and Creator of everything in nature, but the Giver also of grace and glory, the act of love by which for the sake of that same God he esteems His precepts more highly than aught else, and the determination he has formed of losing everything created, and bearing every other misfortune rather than commit a single mortal sin contrary to the Divine commandment, constitute the final disposition for receiving grace, so that this act cannot be performed without supernatural help from God, but the moment it is performed, grace and charity and all other infused virtues are given. Such is the tradition of holy Doctors and sacred Councils, and the sounder and more received teaching of theologians.

It does not, however, follow from this that he who performs this act of love can know with the strictest certainty that he is in a state of grace, since he has no direct and precise evidence of it, but only a strong conjecture constituting a moral probability and certainty. Still, an act of the love of complacency and benevolence, requiring, as it does, for its real completeness a previous act of appreciative love of God, by which grace and charity are acquired, is itself an act and exercise of true charity, and, as we have said, is of great utility and merit.

Christ our Lord has instructed us concerning this act of love. As regards complacency in the excellence of the Divinity, the case is clear, since from the first moment in which the soul of Christ was created and looked upon the Divine Nature, it loved it with a certain kind of infinite love, and delighted itself in all its good, in its every perfection and glory, with a relish and complacency in a measure infinite, since both grace and glory were communicated to it without stint or limit. As regards the complacency of the Soul of Christ in the excellences of the Divinity implanted in creatures, the holy Gospels supply us with several instances. When Christ was first born, the angels that announced His Nativity to the shepherds sang of "*Glory to God in the highest, and on earth peace to men* *of good will."** If the choirs of this Prince were at His bidding to sing with full effect, so as to rejoice the hearts of the friends who came to visit Him, they would require to have carefully learnt beforehand the will of their Prince that they might attune their song according to His desire and intention, and this that heavenly choir of angels had done. First, they saw in the Heart of Jesus that which He wished them to sing, and then they sang, *Glory to God in the highest.* Now, glory is clear perception mingled with praise, and therefore in their lips it meant, May the the glory of infinite Majesty, of infinite goodness, of infinite joy, with highest praise, be to God Who dwelleth in the highest places of Heaven, and may it ever be to God amongst those blessed spirits which are the spiritual heavens, and may these ever praise and glorify Him. It was in this that the angels rejoiced, and desired that it might ever continue; and in this the Heart of Jesus rejoiced, and felt the most supreme delight. "*And on earth peace to men of good will,*" that is, may union of love with God, perfect concord amongst themselves, and rest and calmness of mind under adverse circumstances, be to men who have a deliberate good will towards everything that is right. Thus did the Heart of Christ from the instant of its conception delight itself in that glory which the angels offered to God in Heaven, and desire that all men dwelling upon earth should render Him the same.

Again, when Christ began to preach, He sent His disciples before Him, to declare His Gospel to the cities of Israel, and confirm it with miracles. They did this, reaping a great harvest of souls, and then returned to narrate to their Master what they had done. "*In that same hour Christ rejoiced in the Holy Ghost,*"† that is in the interior of His mind, and with a spiritual joy proceeding from the Holy Ghost, Who dwelt in all fulness within Him, and by argument and word He gave distinct external signs of this joy, thanking His Eternal Father, and saying, "*I con-*

---

* St. Luke ii. 14.   † St. Luke x. 21.

fess to Thee, O Father," I praise and glorify Thee, "*Lord*" and Creator "*of Heaven and earth, because Thou hast hidden these*" so great and profound mysteries, these secrets of the Incarnation of Thy Son, His virtue and merit, the forgiveness of sins, the conversion and salvation of souls, and the general resurrection, "*from the wise and prudent of the world*," on account of their pride, according to the most just judgment and punishment inflicted by Thee when Thy justice shines forth ; and while hiding them from these "*Thou hast revealed them to little ones*," to children in disposition, in the wisdom and influence of the world, in malice, to such as humble and distrust themselves, and submit to be guided by the truths of faith. In two points Christ delighted : one was the salvation and spiritual progress of the souls which received His Gospel, the other was the glory and praise that hence redounded to His Eternal Father.

CHAPTER XXI.

Further examples of the same love of complacency.

IN His discourse on the night of His Passion, after warning His disciples and unfolding many mysteries to them, Jesus added : "*These things*"—that you continue in My love, that you bring forth spiritual fruit, that you keep My commandments—"*I have spoken to you, that My joy may be in you, and your joy may be filled.*"* By which words He meant, My joy rests in the salvation of souls, and the glory of My Father; if you do as I have taught you, this My joy will ever continue, for I shall ever find in you cause and matter for rejoicing, namely, your spiritual and eternal good, and the glory of the Father. That spiritual joy also, which is yours now, shall be carried to highest fulness in the house of My Father, where you shall

* St. John xv. 11.

enjoy along with Me the clear vision of His Divinity. Such was in Jesus Christ the love of complacency in His Eternal Father.

On the other hand, as our Lord rejoiced in the glory and praise which the angels in Heaven and the souls already in possession of faith and charity rendered to His Father, so also He desired that every one on the earth, who as yet had neither love nor faith, might come to the knowledge of Him in faith, and might through love and obedience submit themselves to His law, and honour and glorify Him; and this is the love of benevolence, whereby is desired the true good of the object loved. And our Lord expressed this love when praying to His Father on the night in which He suffered. "*Father, the hour*" of My Passion and Death "*is come, glorify Thy Son, that Thy Son may glorify Thee.*"* As though He had said, Glorify Me in the hearts of men by making it clearly known to the world Who I am, and what I have done for the salvation of the world. And this glorifying, which, O Father, as Man, I seek from Thee, I ask not for Myself, but that Thy Son may glorify Thee; so that when once the mystery of the Incarnation, Passion, and salvation wrought out by Me in the world shall have been manifested to it, Thy Divinity also, Thy goodness, Thy mercy, may become known to it, and Thou Thyself mayest be acknowledged, loved, worshipped, and served by all men.

This is what Christ, as Man, desired and sought after above everything, and to this end He directed His every act and suffering—the praise and glory of His Eternal Father. In this exercise of the love of benevolence we must imitate His example, desiring and promoting in every way the glory and praise of God, and the knowledge and love of Him amongst men. For this object we should expend all our faculties, our labours, and, if necessary, our life itself, saying with the Apostle, "*I am ready not only to be bound, but to die also for the name of the Lord Jesus.*"†

* St. John xvii. 1. † Acts xxi. 13.

To the same great end the Apostle animated and impelled all the faithful, begging them to practise every virtue and to study how to increase therein, doing all for the glory of God. Thus he writes to the Philippians, *"And this I pray"* and ask of God, *"that your charity,"* which is His gift, *"may more and more abound,"* and along with it *"knowledge"* and perfect wisdom, *"and all understanding"*—that is, an experimental knowledge and direction in Divine things, and prudence with respect to the things to be done, *"that you may approve"* and choose *"the better things,"* and more useful to souls, *"that you may be sincere"* in the sight of God, and pure from all fault, and that in the respect of man you may live *"without offence"* to any, but with the edification of all; finally, that you may persevere in these virtues *"unto the day of Christ,"* when He comes to judge you at death, and thus through the virtue and merit of Christ you may in that day be *"filled with the fruit of justice,"* or with works good and acceptable to God, all this tending *"unto the glory and praise of God."* *

Thus far the holy Apostle, who with great reason begs and prays of God that in His servants charity may abound, which is chiefly exercised in the love of God, and in doing everything for His glory. In truth, whoever has a perfect love of God seeks earnestly with his whole heart the glory of God, as the words of St. Diadochus testify in his twelfth chapter: "He who loves God seeks" not his own glory, but "God's, for it is the property of the soul that feels" who God is, "and really loves Him, to be always advancing His glory, but taking pleasure in his own humiliation; because the highest glory becomes a God Who is infinitely great" and infinitely good, "whereas humility" and contempt "belong to man," on account of his vileness and sinfulness.

* Philipp. i. 9—11.

CHAPTER XXII.

Of the care and study with which the Christian should strive to acquire the love of God, and of the effects which this love works in his soul.

OH, of how great import is it that the Christian should apply every faculty of his soul, and should help himself by every grace from Heaven, towards the acquisition of the love of God! For this love consumes in a man all that selfishness which is the root of every evil, it sets him free from his coldness and disinclination for good, from his inordinate affection for creatures, and from the sensual gratification which they afford him; and it makes him diligent in every good work, and in the constant fulfilment of the will of God, and so changes him into a totally different man. As the hard mass of iron, cold, unbending, and sombre in colour, after passing through the fire, comes out heated, glowing like flame, and ready to take any shape desired; so the heart of man, ere it feels any love for God, is cold and immoveable towards good, refuses to obey or to be guided by another, and remains dark and deformed by sin; but the moment that the true love of God finds a way into it, all its coldness and tepidity vanish, it warms up and soon becomes inflamed, it begins to practise virtue with ardour and diligence, it grows gentle and kind towards other men, pliant and obedient to superior authority, bright too and lustrous, and fair to look on, as though already basking in the brightness and beauty of God. Neither the midday splendour wherewith God has clothed the sun, nor the myriad stars with which He has studded the heavens, are so fair or rich an adornment of nature as the Divine love is of the soul of the just man when infused into it by God, and making it to shine forth with Heavenly light. Hence the song of the Prophetess Debbora, "*O Lord, let them that love Thee shine*" with Divine beauty and splendour "*as the sun shineth in his rising.*"*

Another effect of this love is that the observance of the Divine precepts and counsels, most difficult and laborious to the natural strength of man, and in a great degree impossible, becomes through it most sweet and easy. Mere natural and human love renders light and easy the trouble which it instigates a man to take by causing an inclination towards that which has to be done, imparting a relish for it, as we see how light the labour of educating children becomes to mothers, though to others it is unendurable; and again, to those who have a taste for it, the fatigue of fishing or hunting is a pleasure, whereas it is a mere weariness to other persons. As St. Augustine said, "The trouble which those who love put themselves to is no hardship to them, but a delight; for either no labour remains in that which is loved, or else the labour itself is loved."† The same effect is produced in a more perfect and wonderful manner by Divine love. It instils a supernatural inclination towards that which is done for God, and it imparts strength for its execution; it heals corrupt nature, to which good is distasteful as being opposed to its natural tendencies, and enables it to acquire a taste and liking for it. By thus changing the heart, it makes that possible for it which before it could not do, it makes it love that which before it hated, and consider as most light that which was before a most insupportable burden. And this the love of God effects not only as to common labours and ordinary difficulties incident to the observance of precepts and counsels, but also as to very serious undertakings and very grave difficulties, as we see in the case of holy Confessors who found a life spent in practices of most austere penance to be sweet to them, and to whom it

* Judges v. 31. † *Lib. de S. Viduitate*, c. 12.

seemed no difficult matter to watch through whole nights in prayer, to undergo extremes of cold and heat, and in everything to deny their own will, and bend it in obedience to another. All this the love of God wrought in them, for according to the words of St. John, "*This is the charity*" or love "*of God, that we keep His commandments: and His commandments are not grievous*"* to him who has this charity. St. Augustine thus describes this virtue of Divine love and its efficacy, "Nothing is so hard and unfeeling as not to be overcome," made pliant and gentle, "by the fire of love. And when the soul finds itself borne up," by a more than natural love, "towards God," as a bird upon the wing feels not the weight of its body, though perhaps heavy, but flies easily through the air, so it also, by reason of its love "rises freely on its strong and beautiful wings"† above the things of nature in the region of Divine precepts and counsels, until it is united to God in the closest and sweetest embraces of His love.

Yet this love does not only make obedience to God's commands easy and pleasant, but, what is more difficult, it makes light and agreeable the bearing of even pain and adversity, not indeed by the removal of all sense of them, or of that suffering which they naturally cause to us, for in that case much practice of virtue and occasion of merit would be lost; yet it does remove an exaggerated feeling of them, as well as that inordinate sadness, fear, and despair, which do positive harm, and it imparts courage and strength to accept, embrace, and even desire troubles and labours as coming from the hand of God, Who sends them through motives of love, and by their means exercises and increases our love. By which increase of love and diminishing of their natural pain and weight, are augmented the readiness and pleasure with which they are borne. St. Diadochus excellently expresses the same: "As soon as one begins to feel the charity of God strong within him," and those heavenly effects which God is

* 1 St. John v. 3.   † St. Augustine, *Lib. de Moribus Eccles.* c. xxii.

wont to work in great saints, "then does he commence to love his neighbour in and through the Spirit. So that, although there may arise at times some slight irritation in that mind wherein God works, the bond of charity is never broken; for, inflaming itself anew with the heat of the Divine charity, it at once regains the practice of virtue, and with great joy seeks to be in charity with its neighbour, however much contumely or injury it may have received, for it obliterates the bitterness of contention through the sweetness of God."* It prefers the honour and glory of the Divine justice remaining within it, while it itself, for its own demerit, is punished, to all the honours and advantages of the world. It is indeed most fitting that he who is in the state of grace should thus highly esteem the honour of the Divine justice, since it is from it that he hopes to obtain the honour and glory of the eternal life, which, out of the principle of justice, is to be granted to those who love God.

The love of God, in addition, frees the soul from all confusion and excitement, diffusing through it very great calm, peacefulness, and rest, seeing that the true and special home of love is God, and for this end does love exist, that it may all be centred in God, and not extended to any other object unless for the sake of God. As a dislocated arm, forced out of its proper position, cannot find rest from pain till the joint be placed again in its socket, nor the stone lie at rest until the centre of gravity is reached, nor the fire burn quietly unless feeding on the fuel intended for it; so, as long as the love which we owe to God is diverted to any of His creatures, it will always continue restless and fluctuating, until it be restored to God, Who is its true habitation, centre, and sphere. The strict truth of this every man on earth has experienced. For there is no one who has not loved and set his heart on something, and who has not possessed himself of something which he desired; yet all have found that, after

* St. Diadochus, c. xv.

obtaining what they wished, and what they fancied would bring them full satisfaction and content, they were just as restless and dissatisfied as before. Those only have attained true rest of mind in this world who have given all their love to God, loving nothing except God or something for the sake of God, because they only have fixed their love in its proper resting-place, while no one can rob them of that good which they love.

Although it be true that they cannot in this life possess God as perfectly as they desire, yet through love they have begun to possess Him, and this their love makes them hope that they shall enter into full possession of Him in Heaven; seeing Him there in the open brightness of glory Whom they here look upon only with the eyes of faith. This hope fully contents them, and keeps them in a profound peace, for though they greatly long to see Him more clearly and entirely possess Him, yet they love the will of God more than the fulfilment of their own desires, and therefore wait patiently the coming of the time appointed by God, in which they shall see their whole desire fulfilled, and enjoy that infinite Good Whom they love. Of this calm content of those who love God the Psalmist speaks, "*Much peace, O Lord, have they that love Thy law.*"* To love the law of God is to bear Him the love of friendship, since He values more than anything the observance of His law, and they who observe this have peace. What can he, who loves God, desire which he does not obtain? Certainly to him who thus loves, everything is given, nothing is left wanting to him; for whilst he loves the Lord of all, has Him for his friend, and is in full conformity with His will, everything turns to his good, everything helps towards his salvation. Disease itself, loss of means, persecution at the hands of his fellow-men in the cause of God, all these increase his merit, his grace, and his reward of eternal life. His past sins even are turned to profit through the penance that he does for them,

* Psalm cxviii. 165.

through the humility and tender compassion for others that he elicits from them, and through the cautions and warnings by which they teach him prudence as regards both himself and his neighbour. This explains the meaning of St. Paul when he says, "*We know,*" through the teaching of the Divine Wisdom, "*that to them that love God, all things,*" externally or internally adverse to them, "*work together unto good,*" helping to their salvation; and this "*to such as, according to His purpose*" of eternal election, "*are*" in time "*called*" by God "*to be saints*"*— that is, to serve Him in sanctity of life.

O blessed charity! O Divine love! that art of so great value, that dost such wonderful things, and so much exaltest, magnifiest, and honourest those who possess thee! Thou art the regulator of all good actions, directing them towards that highest end, which is God. Thou art the Divine force, giving substance, life, worth, and beauty to all virtues, making them agreeable to God, and worthy of eternal life. It is thou who healest human nature and enablest it to perform those most excellent, high, and supernatural acts which are worthy of the sons of God. Thou art the purest gold of Heaven, enriching souls with gifts of grace and everlasting glory. Therefore it has been justly said of thee, "*If a man should give all the substance of his house,*" all he now has, or shall have, "*in order to acquire the love of God,*" of so great worth and dignity is this acquisition, and such use and benefit does he derive from it, that whatever he may have given for it, "*he shall despise it as nothing,*" as a matter of no price or value, a mere nothing in comparison with the love of God.

* Romans viii. 28.

CHAPTER XXIII.

On the means by which we should procure this love of God, seeking it, desiring it, and eliciting it from all creatures and from all good works.

THE first means to be employed for obtaining the grace of the love of God is earnest prayer from our hearts to God for so great a gift. To this end let us consider well our own weakness and helplessness, which are so great that we cannot do the easiest or simplest good work, nor even desire it, unless moved and assisted by God. And if the work be one which ought to dispose our minds for salvation, the ordinary help of God is not sufficient, His supernatural aid is requisite. How necessary, then, must very especial and very supernatural assistance from God be, when the gift we ask for is one so high and excellent as charity, and when the act to be exercised is that of the supernatural love of God.

Let us consider also that God is most ready to grant us this gift, and is even eager to do so, and thus while confessing our weakness and humbling ourselves on account of it, let us with full confidence in the goodness and liberality of God, pray for this gift with the utmost fervour. St. James himself suggests this means to us: "*If any of you want wisdom, let him ask of God, Who giveth to all men abundantly*" of His benefits and graces, "*and upbraideth not*" for gifts bestowed on faithful and grateful men. "*But let him ask in faith, without wavering*" in doubt as to His power or goodwill to bestow it, "*and it shall be given him.*"* He here calls *wisdom* the gift of the Holy

* St. James i. 5.

Spirit, as being that knowledge of God which springs from the affections of love.

The second means is a fervent and uninterrupted desire to obtain this gift. As the avaricious man eagerly covets money, and the ambitious man honour and high place, so should the Christian be careful to keep alive in his heart an earnest desire to obtain the love of God. And this desire ought to possess his mind, to be present to his memory, to wake him in the night-time, to blend itself with everything he does, as being the first and greatest of all his desires and anxieties. God demands from man a right appreciation of His gifts, that he who receives them should take thought about them and make proper use of them, more especially as concerns this gift of love, which is of all the most excellent. And this deep and constant desire of the love of God springs from the high esteem which a man has conceived for it; and, therefore, God bestows it very willingly and in great abundance upon him who in this manner desires. The Wise Man learned by his own experience that this gift is obtained by earnestly desiring it. Wherefore he says: *"I wished, and understanding was given me: and I called upon God, and the spirit of wisdom came upon me;"** as if he had said, there were given to me understanding enlightened, and a will inflamed, by this gift.

Another very necessary means for the acquisition of the love of God is, that a man should mortify and destroy self-love within him. By self-love is not meant the love by which a man directs himself to God and to that blessedness for which he was created, but the love which a man bears to the things of the world and to any creature merely for his own pleasure, taking himself, not God, for his end and object therein. This love is altogether opposed to the love of God, and is the source of all sins. It must, consequently, be overcome and mortified, that the love of God may be possessed and augmented. St. John, inculcating this, says:

* Wisdom vii. 7.

"*Love not the world, nor the things which are in the world,*" that is to say, riches, honours, pleasures, and all other things which worldly and vicious men love inordinately; for *if any man love* these things, setting his heart upon them and finding his end in them, "*the charity of the Father is not in him.*"*

Another important means is, to try to derive the love of God from all creatures. For which purpose we ought to consider that all creatures are gifts, endowments, costly gems, which God with His own hand sends to us for our help and comfort; and that He sends them to us with love—a love far exceeding in value the gifts themselves, and that His purpose in sending them is to display His love to us and to induce us to love Him. With the same intention, we ought to contemplate the perfections of God as they are exhibited in creatures, and to reflect that every perfection or good quality, which exists in a creature to attract our love to it, is found in infinite fulness in God. If it be the goodness, beauty, and gentleness of a creature which move us to love it, we ought to consider that this goodness, beauty, and gentleness are infinitely greater in God, and have been communicated to the creature by Him. If a man attracts your love by the fact that he loves you and has conferred benefits on you, or that he is your father, or your friend, remember that God's love for you is greater, His benefits more valuable, and that He is more your father and more your friend than any other can be.

Thus should we make use of creatures as instruments for stirring up our hearts to think of God, long after Him, and love Him with our utmost affection. Of this the holy Psalmist sets us the example: "*It is good to give praise to the Lord: and to sing to Thy name, O Most High,*" praising Thy power, Thy goodness, and Thy wisdom. And to this I am moved, because "*Thou hast given me, O Lord, a delight in Thy creating*" of this world, filled with

---
* 1 St. John ii. 15.

so rich a variety and beauty of the creatures made by Thee," *and in these works of Thy hands I shall rejoice,"* contemplating in them Thy power, Thy excellence, and Thy beauty.

The same love we ought to increase through the practice of all virtues and good works, eliciting it from them in these two ways. First, let us in our intentions direct them all to the acquisition through them of God's love, for being done in a state of grace they merit an accession of the love of God, and if in our meditations and the affections of our heart we unite them with the virtues and works of Christ, and then offer them up to the Eternal Father, that for the sake of the virtues of Jesus He may extend His love to us, we shall acquire through them a very great increase of love. In another way we ought to draw more of the love of God from our good works, namely, by doing each act with the consideration that it is God's good pleasure that we should do it, and that He is pleased by it; for it is the part of him who loves to will that which the object of his love wills, to delight and to gratify it, forgetting, at the same time, our own profit, and entirely or chiefly acting in order to conform ourselves to the will of God and to give Him pleasure. In doing this we shall be guided by the true motive and end of the love of God. And these two modes of eliciting love from our exercise of virtues and practice of good works are taught us by the Apostle." *Now the end of the commandment,"* of all the Divine precepts and of the good works by which they are fulfilled, "*is the charity of God proceeding from a pure heart and a good conscience, and an unfeigned faith.*"† And since the end of all the commandments is the love of God, we ought clearly to direct all our good works to the love of God, and perform them for the sake of God.

* Psalm xci. 1, 5.   † 1 Tim. i. 5.

CHAPTER XXIV.

How we ought to learn the love of God from the consideration of Divine things themselves.

THE last and most effectual method of acquiring and increasing the love of God is to contemplate the mysteries themselves of Christ, our Lord, as well as all the other benefits received by us from His hands, the immense love also wherewith He wrought them, and the infinite goodness and mercy that shine forth in every one. For the will is moved to love that which the understanding presents to it as good and deserving of love; and this is what man does in meditating, when he proposes to his will what his mind knows and believes of the goodness of God, of the love which God bears to him, of the good which God has rendered him, and of all the obligations and motives which urge him to love God. And since man does not apprehend the meaning of things at once, as the angels do, but by the gradual exercise of his reason, he ought to weigh slowly and attentively the strongest argument presented to his mind for loving God. Wherefore the word of God and faith in Holy Scripture are called both medicine and seed because they cure our vices and passions, and bring forth virtue and good works. But as no remedy can have any effect unless it be applied to the wound and time be given it to operate, as no seed can produce fruit unless it be sown in the bosom of the earth and be long nurtured within it, so the word of God and faith therein cannot properly heal our vices and passions, nor yet yield the excellent fruit of virtues and holy acts, until the knowledge of what that word says and what faith teaches be fully and deliberately set before the will.

This takes place in mental prayer and in meditation on Divine truths, as David expresses it: "*Thy words have I hidden in my heart, that I may not sin against Thee.*"* To hide the Word of God in our hearts is to turn over in the secret counsels of the soul what the Word of God says and teaches, and the result that proceeds from this is the flight and hatred of sin, which lead to the purity and salvation of the soul. Another Psalm describes this state of the just: "*They are mindful of His commandments, to do them.*"† He is truly mindful of the commandments of God who stores up in his memory all that God has enjoined in His law, and all the motives which should urge him to fulfil it, for it is this fulfilment which constitutes the fruit of good works. St. Bonaventure well describes the process by means of which the mind, in meditating on the Divine mysteries and graces, rises higher and higher, till it attains the perfect love of God and a most blessed peace and tranquillity of heart. He says: " By holy meditation on the things of God, and especially on the love which God has for us, the soul realises all the effects of the Divine sweetness, and thus the love of God grows within it. From this sweetness also arises in the soul a very pressing hunger or ardent desire to possess and fully enjoy in Heaven that infinite good which it already loves and tastes here on earth. Through this longing the love of God grows still stronger in the soul, till it attains the height of a most heartfelt contempt for all the things of earth and an abhorrence of its sensual tastes and pleasures. It turns aside from them all, and can find no relish or pleasant memory except in God, or in those things which bring the soul nearer to God. The same feeling enables it to bear readily the pains and humiliations incident to this life, because they come from the hand of God, Whom it so much loves; it desires to take them cheerfully for His sake, and sometimes even loves and rejoices in them. This again increases the love

* Psalm cxviii. 11.   † Psalm cii. 18.

of God in the soul, which in its turn begets a firm and secure trust in God, owing to the experience which the soul has had of the great favours shown to it by God, Who, for the sake of its love, would gladly bear any injury or ignominy; whence it conceives so assured a hope of Divine assistance as to feel certain this can never be wanting to it, and that it shall never lose either the grace or the love of God."* The result is that a certain wonderful calm dwells in the mind, and, as the Apostle bears witness, "*the peace of God which surpasseth all understanding,*"† every created sense or intelligence, for no power of mere natural understanding can reach unto it nor comprehend either its nature, its value, or its dignity. In this way, however, the servant of God does attain to the perfect love of God through the holy exercise of meditation.

Oh, how great is our happiness in possessing such a gift in this our exile! Oh, how fitting is it that we should give our whole care and labour to the gaining possession by these means of this great good, this infinite treasure, this most sweet and certain pledge of eternal life! Men seek in this world, with the utmost diligence, perishing riches which cannot afford them real pleasure even during life, so great is their mental anxiety and trouble in procuring or else in using them; and when they come to die they are miserable because they cannot take them away with them; nay, the necessity of leaving behind that on which they have set their whole affection is to them an excruciating agony. Some want to have honours and dignities, from which they receive great harm in this life, because they are so unstable and fall into so many sins and errors; and at the moment of death they can get no help from them, but must part company with them all. Others follow more intelligent pursuits; their aim is to become learned in science and in the study of human affairs and natural objects, thus satisfying their tastes and

---

* St. Bonaventure tom. ii. in l. *Parvum bonum*, l. iii. p. 2.
† Philipp. iv. 7.

spreading their fame and their influence; yet, even whilst they live, they draw little advantage from their knowledge, for it teaches them neither humility nor modesty, and it lends no aid at all towards preparing them to make a good death when it comes.

Let us beware of their fatal error and of all that follow their ways, and let us, above everything else, seek the love of God. This will make us just men, perfect in all virtue: it will during this life comfort us in tribulation and strengthen us to surmount our difficulties: it will give us a relish for God and for everything that helps towards our worship of Him: it will preserve us from foolish and exaggerated fears of temporal or even eternal evils: it will establish our minds in great peace and tranquillity; and at the hour of death it will moderate its painfulness, and will refresh and support us with a lively hope of salvation. Nor this alone, for it will, as a most tried friend, accompany us; it will keep us in the sight of God, and will secure our being received by Him with great love as His friends, and as true sons shall we enter on the inheritance of His heavenly kingdom.

CHAPTER XXV.

On the love of charity which we owe to our neighbour, and which should be directed to the good of his soul, not to his mere temporal advantage.

WE have hitherto considered the first and highest exercise of the virtue of charity, namely, the love of God; we now turn to that second exercise of it, which is the love of our neighbour. To make this love a true act of charity it must have the following qualities and conditions. Of these the first is that our neighbour must be loved with a view to the spiritual life of grace and the eternal life of glory, so that the whole of the good desired or procured for him is directed towards making him in this life a just man and true servant of God, and in the next one of the blessed who enjoy God in Heaven for ever. Thus said St. Augustine: "He who rightly loves his neighbour promotes, as far as he can, his soundness of body and his soundness of mind;"* but the diligence wherewith he provides him with what is necessary for the life, health, and commodity of his body aims at securing the health of his mind, that is, his service of God and salvation through Him. Therefore, just so far is he anxious about those things for him which affect his body, as they help to the spiritual and eternal good of his soul, and no further. A man who loves his neighbour, friend, relation, or child, by simply desiring and procuring those things for him which regard the present life, and which enable him to spend it in health, honour, happiness, and pleasure, and who pays no attention to anything necessary for the health and eternal happiness of his soul, nor cares to regulate the temporal advantages he gains for him with any view to his eternal interests, such a man has no real love of charity for his neighbour, but only a human and natural affection.

The same Saint thus speaks of the love of parents, children, and relatives generally: "He loves them according to Christ who assists them to become united to Christ, and heirs with Him of His Kingdom."† In this lies the true love of our neighbour as ourselves, for he alone loves himself in the spirit of charity who loves himself on account of God, and through his love of God desires and possesses for himself that infinite good, which is God. Whence St. Augustine said, "He alone really loves himself who loves God."‡ For this reason the written law did not need to contain a distinct precept of loving oneself, since man by loving God loves himself as he ought, and satisfies the precept of a right and holy love of himself. If a man

---

* St. Augustine, *De Moribus Eccles.* lib. i. cap. xxviii.
† *De Civitate Dei,* lib. xxi. cap. xxvi.
‡ *De Moribus Eccles.* cap. xxvi.

loves only the sensitive part of himself, and provides for it conveniences, honours, gratifications, mingled with many offences against God, and serious injuries to his own soul, he does not really love, but rather hates himself, and is his own deadly enemy. As David said, "*He that loveth iniquity hateth his own soul;*"* and again, the angel Raphael to Tobias, "*They that commit sin and iniquity are enemies to their own soul.*"† Such persons inflict a greater evil and injury on themselves than any enemy can do them, for they cut themselves off from God, they despoil themselves of His glory, and they slay themselves with the death of sin, and of eternal punishment. But he, on the contrary, loves himself with true charity who flies with prompt diligence everything hurtful to his soul, both sin and its occasions, and seeks with most painstaking industry whatever is necessary or useful for the spiritual and eternal good of his soul, such as virtue and sanctity, and the means for obtaining them. Ecclesiasticus thus advises the faithful man: "*Have pity on thy own soul, pleasing God (by a good life), and contain thyself,*" from vices "*Gather up thy heart in His holiness,*" and in purity of life."‡

Since, then, this is the proper love of oneself, it evidently follows that in order to love one's neighbour as oneself, we must help him by our love to serve God and save his soul. St. Augustine declares the same in these words, "He who loves men ought to love them either because they are, or that they may become, just men."§ For a man should love himself just in the same way, and then he can love his neighbour like himself without any danger. Hear St. Augustine in another place: "A man ought to love his neighbour as himself, so as to bring him, either by all possible strength from your help or light from your instruction, or the force of your admonition, to worship God along with you."‖ This duty Christ Himself taught us by His example, as testified by St. Paul: "*Christ also*

---

* Psalm x. 6.   † Tobias xii. 10.   ‡ Ecclus. xxx. 24.
§ St. Augustine, *De Trinit.* lib. ix. cap. vi.   ‖ Epist. lii. *Ad Maced.*

loved the Church, and delivered Himself up for it (in His death); *that He might sanctify it, cleansing it by the laver of water in the word of life;*" by His Blood and the Sacrament of Baptism, and by other appointed means, that after thus sanctifying it on earth He might in Heaven "*present it to Himself* (His spouse and) *a glorious Church, not having spot or wrinkle or any such thing, but that it should be* (altogether) *holy and without blemish.*"*

In order that this holy love of ourselves and of our neighbours may be more perfect, two points must be observed as regards spiritual good and temporal good, regulated according to virtue. The first point is the spiritual benefit, whether of our own or our neighbour's soul; the second is the service and glory of God, in the case of the just and holy man. For if a person desire either of these benefits for himself or for his neighbour, he should do so, not so much for the profit of it to man, as for the service, pleasure, and glory resulting from it to God, the end to whom all your works are to be directed. This Christ intimated in His prayer to His Father, "*Glorify Thy Son, that Thy Son may glorify Thee.*"†

Another mark of the love of charity is that it should be free and liberal, not so much for the sake of the advantage or gain either acquired or to be acquired from it, as because the person benefited is our neighbour, and because it is the will and appointment of God that we should love our neighbour; thus shall we keep ourselves pure from any motives of self-interest. He who loves a neighbour chiefly because he is loved by him, or has received some favour from him, or because he hopes to obtain his love and his good services in the future, does not possess for him the love of charity. Again, if any man loves his neighbour on account of the pleasure and gratification that he feels in his presence and intercourse, as happens with many good persons between whom there is a natural attraction either as to appearance, manner of address, or topics of

---
* Ephes. v. 25—27.   † St. John xvii. 1.

conversation, he does not bear to that person the love of charity. This whole manner of human love, soiled as it is by motives of personal gratification, is a love of concupiscence, and is neither pleasing to God nor meritorious for Heaven. Hence those who give way to it have a vehement affection for some persons, and can feel none towards other persons; and they even lose all their affection for individuals whom they do not see constantly, or whom they find less useful than they had hoped. St. Isidore said, "Those persons are not faithful in their friendship, nor constant in loving, whom interest, not Divine grace, moves to love. For such soon abandon the friend from whom they are not always receiving something, since an affection which is cemented by services rendered is dissolved by the fact of their ceasing."*

The true love of charity is gratuitous; it is not actuated by the desire of temporal gain or advantage, but springs from the love of God, as its fount. And of this nature is the love which a man bears to his neighbour because it is the good pleasure of God that he should love him, and which he thus bears in order to satisfy the love of God that urges him on to love his neighbour; which, in the last place, he bears to him, that by loving his neighbour he may prove his love to God Himself. If a person wishes to excite this love still more in himself by the help of such motives in addition, as the love of his neighbour for him, or the benefit his neighbour has conferred on him, or the hope of some service from him, let him be careful not to dwell too much on these, nor give them too much prominence, but make use of them to go still further, that he may set free his love from self-interest, and entertain it almost wholly for the sake of God. Such is the warning of St. Augustine, "No one can be the true friend of another unless he be first the friend of the eternal truth, namely, God, and of His law; if his friendship is not given gratis, in no way can it be given as it ought."† Therefore this

---

* *De summo bono*, lib. iii. cap. xxx.   † St. Augustine, Ep. lii. *Ad Maced.*

second precept of the love of our neighbour is pronounced by Christ to be like unto the first,* since the two acts of love by which these precepts are fulfilled have but one Father for their origin, namely, God ; and one mother who brought them forth, the virtue of charity, and in loving our neighbour the love of God is practised by loving him for the sake of God. And since on the former precept of the love of God "dependeth the whole law," on it likewise dependeth the second precept of the love of our neighbour.

Christ has taught us by His own example the Divine character of this love, "*This is My commandment, that you love one another, as I have loved you.*"† Though this is an ancient precept, given by My Father under the Law, it is Mine also, laid by Myself on man under My Gospel, and it is a precept to the observance of which I attach especial value. What it enjoins is this, that you should love one another from your hearts, freely and generously, on account of God, according as I have loved you. I loved you before you loved Me, and without any previous worth or merit on your part, or hope of drawing advantage out of you, but solely for your good, and out of love for My Heavenly Father, and because of the glory redounding thence to Him. And I desire and command you to have the same love for each other, without any love or merit in each other going before it, or hope of mutual benefit, but only on account of My good pleasure and of the love which I bear you, and which you all owe to Me. And it is precisely by reason of the example whereby Christ, as Man, confirmed and urged this precept, in loving us so perfectly as He has done, that it is called a new precept. "*A new commandment I give unto you: that you love one another, as I have loved you, that you also love one another.*" ‡

If the owner of some old ancestral mansion were, without destroying the ancient foundations, or any part of the former structure, to raise new apartments and build

---

* St. Matt. xxii. 39.   † St. John xv. 12.   ‡ St. John xiii. 34.

H

a very beautiful wing, and were to make the old part more perfect, laying down new and elaborate pavement, and splendidly adorning the ancient walls, the whole could still be called the old house from the antiquity of its walls and foundations; but it could also be called a new house, or an old house renewed, from the freshness of its additions and rich ornament. The same thing may be said of the commandment to love our neighbour. The command is ancient, given as to its substance and main features by God both in the natural and written law, "*Thou shalt love thy friend as thyself*;"* it is also new, because Christ renewed it, in every respect perfected it, and added many points to its manner of observance which had not existed before. He ordained and promulgated it with the new will which He had as Man, and as being made Man and giving Himself for man, He laid down a new obligation, binding us to its execution. He explained it much more clearly than had ever been done before, showing how this love of our neighbour was commanded with a view to our happiness in the supernatural order, and was to be practised freely and for the sake of God, that it embraced every kind of men, fellow-citizens and strangers, friends and enemies, and should carry us even to the point of sacrificing our life for another if necessary. Christ made it new also in that He taught it to us by his own example as Man, thus instructing us in its method, and drawing us to love in the same manner as He has loved us.

CHAPTER XXVI.

Our love to our neighbour should, especially in cases of necessity, be proved by works.

SOME other qualities of true love for our neighbour are its manifestation by our acts in assisting him when in need, its constancy even to the hour of death, its readiness to undertake great and difficult means of helping him if

* Levit. xix. 18.

requisite, even to the point of abstracting from ourselves what is necessary for our state of life, but not absolutely for our own sustenance, in order to assist him when his need is so great that he would otherwise either soon die, or fall seriously ill, or sustain some other great calamity. This love also requires that in his extreme spiritual necessity, if, for instance, he be involved in some grave error in which he is likely to die and incur eternal damnation, unless he is better instructed and led to correct his sin, we should at once go to his assistance even at the certain peril of our own lives. For, as in his extreme corporal necessity we should place the life of our neighbour before that which befits our own particular state of life, so in the extreme necessity of his soul we are bound to set its salvation above the life of our own body; and if, under such circumstances, we sacrifice our life for another's salvation, great indeed will be our happiness, for we achieve the very noblest act of charity, and shall attain at once to the highest rewards of eternal life. "*Greater love than this no man hath, that a man lay down his life for his friends.*"*

So great love for our neighbour as to give our life for the good of his soul, Christ taught us by His own example, and He calls upon us to imitate Him in similar cases, as St. John likewise exhorts us: "*In this we have known*" the greatness of "*the charity of God, because*," having been made Man, "*He hath laid down His life for us; and we*" therefore "*ought to lay down our lives for the brethren;*"† and this assumes the obligation of a precept, when the soul of our neighbour is in a state of extreme danger. As regards temporal matters the same obligation exists, when the sacrifice of our life is necessary for the safety of the State, or of a Prince on whom the State depends; for then the public good is to be preferred to the life of a particular person.

* St. John xv. 13.   † 1 St. John iii. 16.

CHAPTER XXVII.

In the commandment to love our neighbour the goodness of God and His love towards men especially shine forth.

So high in the law of the Gospel stand the dignity and perfection of this commandment, so wonderful is its force and beauty, with such care for its full efficiency is it promulgated and enjoined, with such strong and weighty arguments is it urged, that man, attentively regarding it in the clear light which God is wont to communicate to faithful souls that are endowed with great charity, sees with the peculiar brightness of faith that it is the law of the true God which contains this great precept, which teaches it, and with such power urges it, and returning fervent thanks to God for giving us this command and praising Him with a heart full of His love, he establishes this precept in his heart, esteems it a most precious treasure of infinite value, and ardently loves it and is resolved to obey it with all diligence. For the soul with great clearness recognizes in this precept the infinite goodness of God, and the immense love and care which He exercises towards every man.

In the first place, it sees that He has made a universal decree for the whole world, requiring all men to love us and to be to us as parents, brethren, guardians, and tutors in doing good to us, in helping us in our necessities, in protecting us from enemies, and from everything else that could injure us, in setting us at liberty, sharing their means with us, and, should it be necessary, sacrificing their very lives in our behalf, whoever we are, as we read in Ecclesiasticus: "*And He gave to every one of them commandment concerning his neighbour,*"* to attend to his good. And

---

* Ecclus. xvii. 12.

this obligation under which all men lie of rendering service to every neighbour cannot be got rid of nor violated, but ever continues, retaining its full strength and energy, as the Apostle reminds us: "*Render therefore to all men their dues. Owe no man anything, but to love one another.*"[*] As we may express it, there is one thing due to all men which still remains owing, though you may have paid it once, and much oftener, and this is the love of your neighbour, together with what it requires, namely, that you succour him in his needs. This debt is never paid off, because you are always bound to it by God, Who commands it and for Whose sake this love must be shown.

In the next place, this precept makes known to us the immense love of God for each one, in that He allows no one really to love Him without at the same time loving his neighbour, whoever he may be. Were it even some great monarch ruling over the whole world who would willingly, for the sake of God alone, without, however, loving his neighbour, expend all his wealth and power, nay, his life, and a thousand lives if he had them, yet God would not accept so great a service, nor would it be pleasing to Him. If that man desires to be really received into God's favour, he must supply the necessary condition, he must love his neighbour, though he were the poorest and humblest upon earth. This St. John clearly intimates: "*If any man say, I love God, and hateth his brother, he is a liar. And this commandment we have from God, that he who loveth God, love also his brother,*"[†] for the sake of God. We have in this precept another proof also of God's great love for each one of us, and of the great pleasure it gives Him to see every one loved and assisted by others, inasmuch as He not only rigidly binds man to love and aid his neighbour, but most highly rewards him for doing this by gifts of grace and temporal benefits which help the soul in this world, and by the eternal riches of His glory in the next.

[*] Romans xiii. 7, 8.   [†] 1 St. John iv. 20, 21.

Nor does God confer only one general reward for love shown and services rendered to a neighbour, but He gives a particular reward for each act of this love and for each benefit which it prompts us to render, a particular increase of grace in this life and of glory in the next; since each good desire and work of charity increases the merit of Divine grace and the reward of eternal glory. Thus St. John: "*He that loveth his brother*" in Christ for the sake of God, "*abideth in the light*," possesses the light of grace and is ruled by it.* And the benefit of that light the same Apostle explains to us: "*If we walk in the light*" of a holy life and conversation, doing those good works that spring from the light of grace, "*as God also is in the light*," and is the Infinite Light itself, "*we have fellowship one with another*" in the same God, are united to Him, and joined together in the closest friendship.† And as a friend, holds intercourse with his friend, reveals to him his secrets, and shares with him his goods; so God holds communion with the just man who loves his neighbour, delights in him, unfolds to him His secrets and mysteries, makes him a partaker of His Divinity, that is, of the beatitude which God Himself possesses, in order that he may enjoy it as far as the creature elevated by the grace of glory can enjoy his Creator.

God so accounts as shown to and done for Him all the love and service extended to a neighbour, that He Himself desires to remunerate and reward it, nor any less reward does He bestow than Himself, the Infinite Good, Who is possessed through grace and eternal glory. And, since there are many who have not been led to love their neighbour, either by the love of God (which they are wholly without), or by the hope of grace and glory (of which they neither feel the benefit nor can appreciate the greatness), God has warned all men that the refusal of their love to a neighbour is a heavy offence against Him, that by this their sin they cut themselves off from His friendship,

* 1 St. John ii. 10.   † 1 St. John i. 7.

His grace, and His glory, and cast themselves into darkness and into the spiritual death of guilt and eternal damnation, and finally that every injury, however slight, done by them in desire or act to a neighbour He takes as done to Him, and will avenge it by temporal punishment in either this or the next life, or if the injury be great, by eternal punishment in the next life. The Evangelist testifies to the strictness of God's punishment: "*He that loveth not*" his neighbour "*abideth in death*," in the death of sin, as regards his soul; and "*Whosoever hateth his brother is a murderer*" in desire; he has neither the life of grace here, nor shall he have the life of glory hereafter.* As long as he remains in so miserable a state, it is evident that he is exposed to damnation, and shall pass through the gate of temporal death into everlasting death.

In this manner Christ has made known to us of what importance with Him is the keeping of this precept, and how greatly He loves every man, and with what powerful sanction of rewards and punishments He commands that all should love one another, excluding no one from the obligation. And, that He might yet more fully declare the tenderness of His affection for the sons of men, He makes fidelity in the observance of this commandment the heavenly sign and seal distinguishing His true disciples from the disciples of the world and of the devil: "*By this shall all men know that you are My*" true "*disciples, if you have love one for another.*"† And since the faithful disciples of Christ are also His brethren and sons of His Heavenly Father, it follows that this same mark of the disciples of Christ is the precious ornament and honourable distinction of the true sons of God, the heirs of His heavenly kingdom, according to the words of the same Apostle: "*In this the children of God are manifest, and the children of the devil,*" through imitation of Him. "*Whosoever is not just*" departing from his sins "*is not*" spiritually born "*of God,*" and so is not His son; and especially he "*that loveth*

---

* 1 St. John iii. 14, 15.   † St. John xiii. 35.

not his brother" is neither just nor the son of God.* From this we are taught that, although the flight of all sin and the fulfilment of all justice are required of the sons of God, it is at the same time their special mark that they fly all hatred or offence of their neighbour and observe carefully the precept of charity.

CHAPTER XXVIII.

God has shown His love to us yet more fully by the new motives for loving one another which He has given us in the Evangelical law.

CHRIST has made still clearer His great love towards man by the fresh reasons which He has given us in His Evangelical law for observing the precept of love to one another. The prophets of old urged men to this love on the ground that all have one God and Father in Heaven, Who created them out of nothing and made their souls after His image. This was the argument of Malachias to the children of Israel, that no man should hate or despise his neighbour, but should love and esteem him. "*Have we not all one Father? Hath not one God created us?*"† To this strong motive Christ added, in the Evangelical law, others still stronger and more efficacious, such as that all men have one Saviour and Redeemer, Who, being the Eternal God and our Creator, assumed our nature, and having thus become Man and our Brother, offered Himself to suffer and die on the Cross, that He might save us from sin and Hell, and might by His gifts of grace reform our souls, that were corrupted and disfigured by sin, and adorn them for His heavenly Kingdom. The points which we have to consider are that this great love and service lay us under the obligation of loving one another, and that Christ

* 1 St. John iii. 10.   † Malach. ii. 10.

requires us to make our return to Him for these and all His other benefits by loving our neighbour for His sake.

St. John declared no less when he said, "*By this hath the charity of God appeared toward us, because God hath sent His only-begotten Son into the world, that we may live by Him;*" whence he argues: "*My dearest, if God hath so loved us, we also ought to love one another.*"* Elsewhere, after saying: "*In this we have known the charity of God, because He hath laid down His life for us,*" he at once infers: "*And we ought to lay down our lives for the brethren.*"† From this passage it is plain that our Lord desires His love and His gifts to be repaid by our loving our neighbour for His sake. To this reason He adds another which is consequent upon it, namely, that all the faithful are members of Christ, and the just are His living members, united to Him by faith and charity; each individual of the faithful represents our Lord so exactly, that every service done to him Christ has considered as done to Himself, from the time that He came into the world clothed with our human flesh. Besides this, all the faithful are parts of the Catholic Church, the Spouse of Christ; they profess one and the same Christian faith; they partake of the same sacraments of grace, and are called to enjoy, in the company of our Lord for ever, that same heavenly inheritance which His merits have obtained for them. St. Paul recounts these motives, and through them urges strongly our love of our neighbour. He thus writes to the Ephesians: "*Careful to keep the unity of the Spirit in the bond of peace.*"‡ Be ye very diligent to preserve that spiritual union which springs from charity, and to preserve it in the spiritual bond of true peace, since you are all members of one mystical body, of which Christ is the Head, and all share in the one Divine Spirit which gives life and movement to the whole body, and so all ought to be of one heart and of one mind, since you are all called by the faith of Christ to the hope of one and the same

* 1 St. John iv. 9, 11.   † 1 St. John iii. 16.   ‡ Ephes. iv. 3.

eternal happiness. Again, afterwards, he exhorts the Ephesians: "*Be ye therefore followers of God, as His most dear children,*" imitate Him in the love which He as Man hath borne us, and that you may do this, "*walk in love*" and grow therein, loving from your heart and doing good to your neighbours, "*as Christ also hath loved us, and hath delivered Himself for us, an oblation and a sacrifice to God* (His Father) *for an odour of sweetness;*"* and this He did that He might satisfy for our sins and reconcile us to God. Wherefore, following the example of Christ, you are bound to love your neighbours, working and suffering for them, and even giving your life for their sake, if requisite.

And since our Lord has thus so greatly extended and perfected this precept of love, showing still more the love of God for us, and has confirmed our obligations to obey it, inciting us thereto by many motives for the greater spread of fraternal charity in the world, we cannot but see most clearly that the law of the Gospel is the true law of God. This same precept was contained in God's natural law and in His written law, and God then showed in it His love, and, by motives sufficiently strong, bound man to its performance; and yet the fruit reaped from it was but small, since few really loved their neighbours perfectly. To whom, then, should we look for its renewal and greater effect, if not to God Himself, Who gave it? Neither the devil, nor bad men, his ministers, could do this; for the devil, in his enmity and malice against man, has ever been, as Christ called him, "*A murderer from the beginning of the world, and he stood not in the truth.*"† The devil has been a slayer of man's soul and of his body, and though created in the truth, with power to know and virtue to follow it, he did not persevere, but lost all grace and became a liar, and the father of lies.

It is evident, therefore, that He who was to perfect this commandment must be God, Infinite Goodness, and that the instruments which He was to employ must belong to

* Ephes. v. 1. † St. John viii. 44.

Him and act by His power; such were the Sacred Humanity of Christ, and His Evangelical law, and also the disciples whom He chose. This argument has by itself such evident force and truth that he who can thoroughly examine it by the help of Divine light, would see by it how truly the Evangelical law is the law of God. Thus many holy men have received this especial gift from God, that, along with faith in those supernatural mysteries which the Evangelical law teaches, they have seen clear evidence that the law embracing such mysteries was the law of the true God; while those not so especially enlightened from Heaven can at least be led by this argument to see that the Evangelical law is most worthy of belief, and is to be believed and received as the most holy law of God.

Now, though it be true that every precept of this law, if well considered in that purity and perfection in which the teaching of the Gospel has handed it down, and with which the great saints of the Church have practised it, has the same weight that we have given to this one in particular, yet, because this precept of loving our neighbour for the sake of God is chief of all, and virtually includes the whole law, and because its fulfilment conduces most to the good of the world and is most obvious to the eyes of men, it has greater influence and effect in imparting a clear and general insight into the holiness, truth, and excellence of the complete Evangelical law. Wherefore our Lord in His prayer to His Heavenly Father, beseeching Him to grant to His faithful the execution of this precept, or the union of all in charity, pronounced this to be the testimony that should move the world to believe in Him: "*Holy Father, keep them in Thy Name whom Thou hast given Me, that they may be one*" through faith and charity, "*as we also are one*" in nature: "*that the world may believe that Thou hast sent Me.*"* Thus men who were without faith and were lovers of the world, on beholding the wonderful union

---
* St. John xvii. 11, 21.

effected by perfect charity amongst the faithful, would be moved to believe in Him Whom the same faithful confessed and adored as their Saviour, the true Son of God, and God Himself, sent by the Father to assume a mortal body and to save the world.

CHAPTER XXIX.

Examples, by which Christ has taught us the love of our neighbour, infusing that love into all who come to Him and believe in Him.

HAVING up to this point considered in what consists the love of our neighbour springing from true charity, as well as the perfection of the precept enjoining it, and the arguments and motives urging us to its fulfilment, let us now dwell on some examples in the life of Christ whereby He taught and recommended to us the love of our neighbour. This He did when He at once moved those who approached Him and conversed with Him and heard His word to exercise this love, procuring the good of their neighbour's soul, and the good of his body also, as far as conducive to the spiritual good of his soul.

St. Andrew followed Christ, stirred to do so by the testimony of St. John the Baptist. And after he had remained with Christ one night, he sought on the next day Simon Peter, his brother, saying to him : " *We have found the Messias, which is the Christ,*" promised under the law ; "*and he brought him to Jesus,*" Whose disciple he became.* Christ called Philip, and took him to be His disciple. Philip soon found his friend Nathanael and told him : " *We have found Him of Whom Moses in the law, and the Prophets did write, Jesus the Son of Joseph of Nazareth:*"† and he led him to Jesus, that he might learn the truth from Him. Now, that St. Andrew after one night's converse with our Lord is filled with a strong desire to

* St. John i. 41.   † St. John i. 45.

find his brother, that he goes forth to seek him with the utmost diligence until he finds him, that he persuades him with all fervour to come to Christ, to accept Him as his Master and believe in Him as the Messias; again, that Philip too, after hearing and being drawn sweetly to Christ, immediately went in search of Nathanael, assured him with such firm conviction that Jesus was the promised Saviour, and urged him with such charity to submit himself to the teaching of the same Lord—these are proofs furnished to us by Christ Himself that what He taught those coming to Him and choosing Him as their Master, was that true charity which filled them with the love of their neighbour and with the desire to procure the salvation of his soul. This St. Chrysostom points out: "Andrew did not confine to his own breast that which he learnt from Christ, but went at once with all speed to his brother, and through charity communicated to him the discovery which he himself had made."* "And this," says Bede, "is truly to find Christ, to burn with the true love of Him, namely, to have a care also of our brother's salvation." †

Christ called St. Matthew from the receipt of custom and moved him to repent of his sins. He took away from his heart all greed of earthly gain, filling him with spiritual joy and the love of heavenly treasures, together with the hope of obtaining them, so that, in the ardour of Divine love now inflaming his heart, he desired that all his friends should participate in his happiness.‡ For, on seeing many following him because he himself had come to Christ, he "made a great feast," inviting our Lord to it, and he asked to it all his friends who were publicans and sinners like himself, that they might see our Lord at his table, might draw near to Him and hear His words, and being thus moved to penance might lay aside the covetousness that kept them ensnared in sin, and might obtain true consolation and come to share in that blessing which he

---

* St. Chrysostom *in Joan.* i. hom. 18, 19.
† Bede, *Serm. de Sanctis.*   ‡ St. Mark ii. 14, 15.

then enjoyed. This, again, was true fraternal charity which Christ teaches all those who follow Him, and with which they themselves being set on fire, inflame other souls also with the love of virtue and of heavenly gifts.

When Christ accompanied by His disciples had crossed the Sea of Galilee, He landed on the shore of Genesareth, and after He had begun to preach and to incite the crowds by His presence and words to the desire of heavenly things, their hearts were inflamed with such an ardent fraternal charity that, "*Running through the whole country, they began to carry about in beds those that were sick. And whithersoever He entered they laid them in the streets, and besought Him that they might touch but the hem of His garment: and as many as touched Him were made whole.*" * At another time when our Lord was not far from the Sea of Galilee, "*Going up into a mountain He sat; and there came to Him great multitudes;*" to whom He taught His heavenly doctrine. These also, stirred with brotherly love, brought to Him from the villages all kinds of sick persons, "*the blind, the lame, the maimed, and many others; and they cast them at His feet,*" and our Lord at once healed them all, "*so that the multitudes marvelled seeing the dumb speak, the lame walk, the blind see; and they glorified God.*" † Thus does Christ also communicate to those who follow Him and listen to His word the charity of assisting their neighbours with great diligence in things necessary for preserving their corporal life and conducive also towards their spiritual good, similar to the healing of their bodies which He wrought upon the sick; since through that He incited them, as far as possible, to penance for their sins and amendment of life, and so to those who obeyed His Divine inspirations He gave the healing of their souls as well as of their bodies.

Our Lord did not always propose the same works of charity in those who followed Him, but varied these, and changed from one to the other even on the same day,

* St. Mark vi. 55.   † St. Matt. xv. 30.

as St. Matthew and St. Mark point out. After He had ceased preaching He came into the coasts of Peræa, and great multitudes followed Him, and according to His wont He taught them again, and also healed the sick. Then He replied to a question put by the Pharisees, and having satisfied them, afterwards instructed His disciples, privately expounding to them the counsel of chastity. This exhortation finished, He blessed the little children brought to Him; after which He explained all that was necessary for attaining salvation and perfection to the young man who came and asked Him, what he should do to receive everlasting life; then He again spoke to His disciples in private and gave them the counsel of evangelical poverty.*

Thus, in another way, Christ taught us how to exercise ourselves in many and various works of charity to our neighbour, according to our talent and ability, in order that we may render him more help in his needs and supply him with the particular remedy which he requires, and that we may practise several different virtues and good works, assisting one another in them. So that, after rest has been given to the mind during the performance of some corporal act, a return to prayer, or reading, or teaching will enable us to perform that spiritual duty with greater diligence and success. Then, again, if after prayer, or reading, or instruction for the good of a neighbour we turn to the performance of some external work of charity, we perform it with more devotion, and avoid that feeling of fatigue which the continuance of one and the same occupation, however good or useful, in our present state of weakness necessarily brings on. St. Chrysostom remarks this of our Lord: "He did not confine Himself to constant instructions or exhortations, nor yet to the constant working of miracles, but He changed from one to the other that He might do good in many different ways. Thus His teaching appeared all the more worthy of belief through the greatness and number of His

* St. Mark x. i.

miracles; while on the other hand, the effect of His miracles was made more abundant by His preaching and doctrine."*

CHAPTER XXX.

A particular example given to us by Christ of honouring our neighbour on festive occasions.

Our Lord's condescension in accepting the invitation sent Him to be present at the marriage feast in Cana of Galilee, and in kindly adapting Himself to the customs of the poor and simple people who had asked Him, His honouring them with His presence and coming to their aid by working His first miracle, these acts teach us the charity we should practise in going to the houses of our neighbours, in honouring and sympathizing with them on such festive days as the birthdays of their children, their marriage-day, or if a friend be saying his first Mass, or on the occasion of a college feast, at funerals also, and on any other similar day on which our neighbour is wont to be visited by his friends. For we should show to others befitting respect in everything that is right and lawful, since charity is thus preserved and increased; and when such little attentions are paid to them, neither through human respect nor for selfish ends, but in the spirit of charity and of compliance with the will of God, our acts are meritorious and highly agreeable to Him. This is taught us in the example set us by our Lord, for He both ordained that He should be invited, and after accepting the invitation, He favoured the nuptials by working a very celebrated miracle.

And the like favour should princes and persons of rank accord, not merely to their equals, but still more to the simplest and poorest, and very especially to persons set aside and neglected by others; for in such cases,

* St. Chrysost. *Matt.* xix. hom. 63.

wherein neither human respect, nor chance of recompense, nor a temporal return of any kind can be the motive, charity is more exclusively observed and the act more grateful to God. Since then Jesus Christ in His infinite Majesty did not disdain to enter the house of such humble and needy persons, that He might honour them by His Divine presence, it becomes no man, however great in the world's eye he may be, to refuse a similar office of charity to any persons who may ask it of him, so long as it does not involve too serious an inconvenience. To deny the courtesy as being too exacting or below one's dignity would be a mask of pride, as St. Augustine observes in these words: " Let a man feel shame at being proud, since God made Himself humble by assuming our human nature." *

CHAPTER XXXI.

An example set us by Christ of helping our neighbours in their necessities.

WHEN our Lord sent the twelve Apostles to preach throughout the land of Israel, and on another occasion the seventy-two disciples, He did not bid them go forth singly, but two by two. When He sent His disciples to bring the ass and its colt for His use in entering Jerusalem, though one messenger would have been sufficient, He sent not one only, but two. By these acts He taught how much He desired, and how much it pleased Him that one neighbour should succour another in all temporal and spiritual matters, and that every one should exercise charity. For when two go together the one assists and strengthens the other, if one falls, the other helps him up; if one grows weary, the other supports him; if one does too much in his zeal, or abstains too long, the other keeps him in kindly check, makes him take more rest, and eat what is neces-

* St. August. *De verbis Dom.* serm xli.

sary for his sustenance; if one be remiss and negligent, the other corrects his fault; if one is tempted by an enemy to any unworthy action, the fear of the other's presence deters him; if one is in a state of doubt as to what he should do, the other is close at hand to assist him by his counsel.

Besides this, when two are together, each is a faithful witness to the other's purity and rectitude of conduct, both in his mode of life and fulfilment of his several duties, who can give testimony in his favour, and exonerate him entirely from that suspicion, from which he could scarce have cleared himself if alone.

Such as this is the charity which Christ wishes us to practise towards each other, giving mutual help both in temporal and spiritual affairs. And that He might the better instruct and persuade us thereto, He directed His disciples to go out in companies of two instead of singly. What He taught by act during His mortal life He had even before that taught in Scripture by His Holy Spirit. "*It is better therefore that two should be together, than one; for they have the advantage of their society,*" if both be of virtuous life. "*If one,*" by any external calamity or danger, or by any spiritual sin or temptation, "*fall, he shall be supported by the other. Wo to him that is alone,*" or to whom good companionship is wanting, "*for when he falleth he hath none to lift him up,*"* no virtuous companion to do so. The same Holy Spirit tells us in the Book of Proverbs, "*A brother that is helped by his brother is like a strong city,*"† for when the citizens help one another, their town is better defended and strengthened.

Let us confirm this truth by the following instances from the lives of the saints. Palladius tells us of a very holy monk, of the name of John, a great lover of solitude, who was so dear to God, and so tenderly cherished by Him, that he received from God through an angel the bread by which he was fed. Growing elated at so singular

* Eccles. iv. 9.   † Prov. xviii. 19.

a privilege he began to trust in himself, and on one occasion gave the enemy such an opportunity of plying him with a very strong temptation that, overcome by it, he decided on quitting the holy life which he led, on returning to the world, and giving himself unrestrained to his desires. When on his way, he turned aside to a certain monastery to rest from the fatigues of his journey, and was received with great charity by the monks. After some spiritual conversation he was requested to give them an exhortation on the mode of overcoming the temptations of the devil. Not daring to refuse, he began his discourse, and then turning his thoughts inward he perceived the terrible fault into which he had fallen; he was seized with penitence for his sins, returned to his solitude, and there in the austerity of the rest of his life he expiated the serious fault he had committed. In this monk were, as Palladius says, fulfilled the words of Scripture which we have quoted, "*A brother that is helped by a brother is like a strong city.*"

St. Basil and St. Gregory of Nazianzen were very great friends, and lived together in retirement and in the study of literature, each receiving the greatest profit from the other's companionship and intercourse. They were able to live so long in this union and fellowship, and to draw so much fruit from it, because, as St. Gregory tells us, the one not only always studied how to assist and oblige the other, but also yielded to him in every respect the first place, the most honour, and the best things he could. And in this mutual emulation and contention neither would take the best for himself, but on the contrary, what was most laborious, most difficult, and most unassuming, and by this exercise of humility and charity on both sides they became of one heart and of one mind, such rich fruit of spiritual grace did they receive through each other's society. This example of two great Saints should be copied by all desirous of living in union with their neighbour who serves God, that they may maintain this union, and draw benefit from intercourse with him. For where each one seeks what best suits himself, what is most to his taste and corporal ease, all pleasure in spiritual friendship is at an end, mutual charity is chilled and dried up, and no further fruit can be gained from mutual intercourse. But if each one be willing to cede to his companion that which is best and most valuable, the pleasure of friendship is revived, charity between both is increased, and great fruit is gathered in from their mutual friendship and society.

And this rule of yielding to the other still holds good, though it be observed only by one side, nay, in this case charity and humility are more fully practised. If but one keeps the law of charity, and the other refuses to observe it, so that, while one yields to the other the first and best of everything, the other refuses ever to return his act of love, even then the former loses nothing really, nay, he gains so much the more, since his exercise of charity becomes all the purer, the inconvenience to himself makes it the more generous, and it is far more agreeable to God. And this sacrifice can be most easily made by the true servant of God, who for the sake of God loves his neighbour without seeking return, nor desires in the charity which he practises aught else than to please God, and attain to perfect virtue and his eternal good; while this object before him is little affected by the fact that the other will not respond to his act of true charity. Rather indeed is he the gainer, since the other has enriched him with matter and opportunity for pleasing God more abundantly, and for meriting a nobler reward from Him.

This exercise of charity, whereby we choose for ourselves what is most troublesome, most lowly and humiliating, is also taught us by our Lord's own example, as St. Paul wrote to the Romans. "*Let every one of you please his neighbour unto good, to edification,*"* that is, in what is good and praiseworthy, not in order to obtain the honour and favour of others, in which men delight, but for their edification

* Romans xv. 2.

and greater building up in the faith and love of Christ. And what should nerve us to this is that Christ, Whose example we are bound to follow, "*did not please Himself,*" by making choice of that which would bring greater consolation and utility to Himself, or temporal ease to His most Sacred Body, or satisfaction to His own natural will. So far from that He, to do His Father's will and serve our needs, chose what was most opposed to His own comfort and natural desire, for the Psalm of David represents Him thus addressing His Father, "*The zeal of Thy house hath eaten Me up, and the reproaches of them that reproached Thee are fallen upon Me.*"* The reproaches of impious men amongst God's people of Israel, who had by word and act denied the truth of God, had fallen upon Christ, because when He declared to that same people the will of the Father, and accused them of their sins, they attacked Him also with reproaches and injuries, and were resolved to take His life. The iniquities with which all men had offered violence and insult to His Heavenly Father were fallen upon Christ, Who had to sustain the punishment due to each one of them.

Animated by this example of our Lord each one should resolve to choose for himself whatever is most inconvenient and most opposed to his own private taste, that there may be good fellowship and true union between him and his neighbour. We are not, however, to fall into the mistake of condemning the practice of the holy anchorets and others, who imitated Christ in following a solitary life, and served God with great perfection in the desert; for although Christ taught, and Holy Scripture affirms, that it is safer and better for two at least of the servants of God to be together, yet there is no general rule which does not admit of some exceptions. And in the present case, when God grants an especial vocation to a solitary life, and gives at the same time the virtue and disposition of mind and recollection in prayer specially suited to that

* Psalm lxviii. 10.

life, He supplies amongst these all the benefit and advantage which the mutual society of good men affords. Indeed, He supplies this most plentifully, as the lives of many holy hermits bear witness, who shine forth brightly amongst the other saints of the Church, both for their sanctity and the good they did to others by their example and their prayers.

But inasmuch as by no means all are called to be solitaries, while few have the virtue and the grace necessary for that life, it may not be embraced without much consideration, nor without the advice and approbation of persons of prudence and tried virtue. Another point is that they who live much in the company of other servants of God on account of the benefit and the protection which it is to them, are not to be always and in every spiritual work associated with others, but only at certain times and in certain exercises which require or admit of it. There are both seasons and duties in which they should be alone and at perfect rest, for the sake of prayer, recollection, contemplation, the interior perception of heavenly truths, and that they may practise those penances which it is not becoming for others to see. Hence those saints who speak much in praise of the mutual intercourse of holy men, and who have themselves greatly benefited by it, show their esteem also for solitude, and the good they have derived from it. Amongst whom we may quote St. Gregory Nazianzen in his *Apology*, "I embrace solitude and take her for my companion, as a spiritual mother who strengthens me much in raising my mind to God, and in holding communion with His Divinity."*

St. Chrysostom likewise felt greatly the advantage of the union of solitude with the society of the good, and thus speaks of his experience, "Solitude has filled the just with many blessings in this life, and in their departure out of it solitude has led them forward bright and full of joy

---

* St. Greg. *In Apolog.* 2 *ad Julian.*

to the judgment-seat of God," through the sure pledge which they have of their salvation, and their strong and certain hope of the fruition of the Divine glory.

CHAPTER XXXII.

Fraternal charity requires the faithful to console one another in their distresses, as we see from the examples given of our Lord.

IT is the part of fraternal charity to help our neighbours in their misfortunes, pains, and afflictions. Christ did this, and He has instructed His followers to do this also. When He saw that the multitude who had followed Him into the wilderness were wearied by much walking and standing during His sermons and miracles, and that hunger also was added to their fatigue, He not only gave them to eat, but told His disciples to make them sit down amongst the soft grass. On both occasions of His miraculously feeding them He showed the same care for them. And when His Apostles returned from preaching throughout the towns of Israel, and recounted to them all that they had done, in order to refresh them after their exhausting labours, He said to them: "*Come apart into a desert place, and rest a little.*"*

In these instances Christ has given us proof of the tenderness of His charity, and shows that, although for those who serve Him He ordains trials and difficulties on their path to Heaven, in order to increase their virtue and merit, yet He also soothes and comforts them lest they should succumb under suffering, or fail to understand the love that sends it for the greater good of their souls, and not for the sake of refusing them all consolation. In these instances He has also made known His will that those,

* St. Mark vi. 31.

who are occupied in His service and for His sake ar practising themselves in acts of virtue, should at the proper time take necessary and befitting rest, and such recreation as becomes their state, for without these nature is over fatigued and their spirit is depressed, and they require to gain fresh strength for renewing the work before them. He has thereby taught us also to extend the like charity to our neighbours, especially our dependants and domestic servants, loving them as brethren and members of Christ, feeling for them and affording them comforts, little alleviations, and rest from work when they are suffering; showing charity in the same way to our guests or to strangers, providing whatever is necessary for them, that they may rest from their journey and fatigue, and may have the benefit of such attentions and indulgences as charity should show them. As St. Theophylact remarks, "Christ teaches us by His example that whenever we receive a guest into our house we ought to give him full opportunity of resting, sitting for some time, or sleeping, or of receiving from us whatever else may in reason be deemed necessary for his refreshment."*

Christ has given us other examples of the same charity, by consoling His followers in their distress and affliction. When He began to unfold to His disciples some of the mysteries and events of His Passion, such as that "*He must go to Jerusalem,*" to be "*delivered to the Gentiles,*" to be "*mocked, and scourged, and spit upon, and to be put to death,*" He at the same time added that all these sufferings and afflictions should have a speedy and glorious end when "*the third day He should rise again,*" and enter into possession of His eternal glory.† He forewarned them, indeed, of His Passion and Death, for it was requisite they should know of these beforehand, that when they took place they might remember and fully acknowledge how voluntarily He had given Himself up to death for the salvation of the

---

* Theophyl. on St. Luke ix.
† St. Matt. xvi. 21 ; St. Luke xviii. 31, 33.

world; yet, wishing to moderate their grief on hearing these tidings and to console them in their distress, He at once pointed out the glory which His Passion and Death would secure for Him, as well as the fruit of eternal salvation which they would bring to the world. Thus in the moment itself of causing His servants a great sorrow, He convinces them that His motive is not simply to distress them, but for the sake of the fruit to be reaped from it, namely, God's glory and the good of their own souls. And therefore does He remind us of those happy and blessed results which, both in this life and the next, follow upon trials submitted to for the sake of God, in order to make those same trials easier and sweeter to us, and enable us to endure them with greater consolation.

That which our Lord has done, He wishes us likewise to do. When, therefore, He sent His disciples to preach repentance, sorrow for sin, and mortification of the flesh in satisfaction for sin, He bade them preach at the same time and announce the remission of sin, the Kingdom of Heaven, and the resurrection of the body to a life of glory. He wished that the grief and sadness caused in men by penitence and dread of the Divine judgments should be assuaged by those better tidings, and cheered by the high and glorious hopes which they inspired, declaring to men that the Kingdom of Heaven was in very truth everlasting, that their sins were done away in their penance for them, and the way to Heaven opened out, that God Himself promised them pardon, and invited them to enter His Kingdom. This direction the Apostle St. Peter carried out to the letter. For when in discoursing to the Jews he had penetrated them with a most anxious fear and grief for having crucified their Saviour, and they cried out to him and to the rest of the Apostles: "*Men and brethren, what shall we do?*" He immediately reassured them, saying: "*Do penance, and be baptised every one of you in the Name of Jesus Christ;*"* thence you shall at once receive

* Acts ii. 37, 38.

"*the remission of your sins and the gift of the Holy Ghost*," as the grace and pledge, or assurance, of eternal happiness.

We have an example of the same in St. Paul, when addressing the Jews; for after he had filled their hearts with grief and shame by the recapitulation of their crime in desiring of Pilate that they might put our Lord to death, he instantly burst out into the declaration, "*Be it known to you, men and brethren, that through this same Lord forgiveness of sins is preached to you*,"* and to all who believe in Him with a lively faith. And what he did by word of mouth, that he also did when writing to the Thessalonians: "*This we say unto you in the Word of the Lord*," that when the Lord shall come down from Heaven to the universal judgment, then all, both "*they who have slept*" and "*we who are alive*," shall rise again. They indeed who shall have died before that day, if they have departed this life in the faith and grace of God, shall rise to the life of glory first, and after they "*who are alive, who are left, shall be caught up to meet Christ.*" Then shall all the just be taken up together amid the clouds into the air to meet Christ our Lord, and He will then receive us into His glorious company and conduct us to His Heavenly Kingdom, where, glorified and beatified in body and soul, we shall for ever be living and reigning with the Lord. "*Wherefore comfort ye one another with these words.*" †

It is after this manner that Christ wishes us to comfort one another in our several misfortunes and afflictions by good works and holy words, for this does fraternal charity require of us. Thus the same Apostle enjoins us: "*And we beseech you, brethren, rebuke the unquiet,*" who are living without Christian regularity or discipline; "*comfort the feeble-minded,*" who succumb to their trials and place but little trust in God; "*support the weak,*" protecting and assisting them both in body and soul, that, like parents and spiritual physicians, you may restore and heal them.‡ Let us observe that as the charity, which moves us to love

---
* Acts xiii. 38. † 1 Thess. iv. 14—17. ‡ 1 Thess. v. 14.

our neighbour is to be directed to the spiritual and eternal good of his soul, so also that consolation which we strive to give by word and by deed in things temporal ought also to help to the spiritual good of his soul. For, while we seek to comfort him, we must not benefit his body in a way that exposes him to the danger of sin, nor may we so speak to him as to run the risk of favouring or feeding the vice and passion he may be subject to; nor can any truth be justly kept from him which it behoves him to know, nor any correction spared of which he stands in need. For the example of our Lord instructs us on all these points.

Whilst Christ was staying in the house of Martha and her sister Mary, Martha, as mistress of the house, "*was busy about much serving*," and about procuring the things necessary and worthy of so great a Guest, in which work she was not a little anxious and fatigued. In her over anxiety she approached our Lord, seeking help in these words: "*Lord, hast Thou no care that my sister hath left me alone to serve*," and she who ought to share the burden sits idly at Thy feet? "*Speak to her, therefore, that she help me.*" Now, though Martha was thus wearied and distressed in so good an action and with so holy an intention, yet Christ refused her all consolation, either by approving her complaint, or passing her fault over in silence, or bidding her sister to go to her assistance.

If as Man He had been guided by mere human feeling, He would have taken up her quarrel, and said: "Martha, in My care for you I highly esteem your service and your very great diligence; your request is fair, and your sister ought at once to help you, that the labour may be divided, and both may partake in the merit of so good an action." This is what some kind-hearted person would have replied, had he thought more of Martha's temporal consolation than of the spiritual good of her soul. But Christ, her Heavenly Master, looking more to her spiritual need, did not thus comfort her, but humbled and corrected her, and made her see her mistake. Approving of the work in itself, He found fault with her needless anxiety and distress of mind in these words: "*Martha, Martha, thou art careful and art troubled about many things.*"* It was as if He had said, "Though the active life, which thou hast chosen in performing the external works of charity, is good and pleasing to God, yet the contemplative life, of which Mary hath made choice, is better, more excellent, and more pleasing to God, since in it the interior love of God is more fully exercised." So did our Lord treat Martha, not giving her the consolation which she asked for, nor saying those things to her which would fit in better with her state of mind at the time, and with the mere human motives under which she was then acting; but He strengthened her with that true consolation which was more useful for her soul, and which would build it up and advance it in spirit.

And He would have all treat their neighbours in the same way; consoling them, indeed, when in affliction, and strengthening them both by word and deed, yet at the same time directing all this consolation to the spiritual and eternal benefit of their souls, as being the true end of charity. St. Paul sums up this matter admirably when he says: "*In all things let us exhibit ourselves, as the*" faithful "*ministers of God.*"† Then, after enumerating many virtues by the practice of which we shall prove ourselves to be such ministers towards our neighbours, he commends to us "sweetness," that, for example, in dealing and conversing with them we should not be rough or morose in our words or actions, but kind and gentle, accommodating ourselves to each one's dispositions and ways, that so we may console all; doing this "*in the Holy Ghost*," that is to say, not according to motives of mere human affection, which has one's own temporal good only in view, and humours our neighbour in what is unlawful or injurious to his soul, but according to the Spirit as being His gift. Our "sweetness," therefore, should proceed from the love of God, and

* St. Luke x. 38, seq. † 2 Cor. vi. 4, seq.

be exercised under the suggestion and guidance of the Holy Spirit, who seeks the glory of God and the spiritual good of our neighbour.

CHAPTER XXXIII.

In our exercise of charity to our neighbour we must necessarily bear with his faults, and must sacrifice no little of our own convenience. Examples of this in the life of Christ.

SINCE in our exercise of charity to others we cannot but encounter much inconvenience, annoyance, and difficulty; and since many, to avoid these, either omit its exercise altogether or carry it out so inefficiently as to rob their actions of all merit, Christ teaches us by His own example how true charity accepts the inconvenience and overcomes the difficulty. St. Luke relates that, when our Lord stood near the Lake of Genesareth, the great multitudes which gathered round to see Him and hear His Divine Word, "*rushed in upon Him*" like waves dashing up against the rocks.* St. Mark likewise describes how, as Christ was working miracles on the sea-shore and healing many by the touch of His most Sacred Body, a great multitude of all sorts came from Judæa, Idumea, Tyre, and Sidon, and amongst them many that had wounds and diseases crowded round Him so excitedly to touch Him that they pushed against Him, and seemed as though they would force Him into the water.† Again, when our Lord passed through the streets on His way to heal the ruler's daughter, so large a number were waiting to see Him in addition to those already following after Him, that their pressure was painfully felt by His delicately sensitive Body. The pressure of this crowd gave opportunity to the woman afflicted with an issue of blood to touch His garment without being seen by any one. To our Lord's question, "*Who is it that touched Me?*" His Apostles replied: "*Master, the multitudes*

* St. Luke v. 1.   † St. Mark iii. 10.

throng and press Thee, and dost Thou say, Who touched Me?"* Such inconveniences as these Christ endured from men with so great interior and exterior charity, that He neither complained, nor spoke sharply to them, nor showed Himself vexed even by the expression of His countenance, but bore all in silent patience, and with calm and smiling face. He did not omit a single act of charity, nor did He shorten it, but continued to the end doing good to all; this, according to St. Paul, is the character and mark of true charity, that it is patient and enduring.

These examples teach us to allow neither our patience nor our charity to be overcome, however much our neighbour may vex and distress us by his importunity or obstinacy, by his blundering questions, or long, unmeaning stories, his cunning, his lies, and his rude or selfish behaviour; on the contrary, we must calmly and unflinchingly persevere in doing good and in enduring evil, and must refrain from all anger, excitement, or hasty language. By such conduct as this our true and solid charity manifests itself, and by willingly enduring what is so hard to bear it is greatly strengthened, and shines forth purer and more perfect; it is more pleasing to God, and richer in merit for ourselves. Hence St. Gregory maintains that the proof of sanctity is not the power to work miracles, but the possession of charity, whereby we love our neighbour as ourselves.† To the question, What is the proof of this love? he answers: In the same proportion that a person loves does he bear with his neighbour; for if you love, you bear gently with him whom you love; and you cease to bear kindly with another when you cease to love him.‡

St. Paul thus exhorts all the faithful: "*I beseech you that you walk worthy of the vocation in which you are called*;" that you may be members of Christ, "*in all humility and mildness, with patience, supporting one another in charity.*"§ He would have us bear with one another's hard and rough

---

* St. Luke viii. 45.   † St. Gregory, lib. vii. *Moral.* cap. x.
‡ Hom. xv. *in Ezech.*   § Ephes. iv. 1, 2.

ways, with those faults into which all are apt to fall, with the injuries to which we may be exposed, so that neither from passion or indiscreet zeal we suffer anger or indignation to arise within us, nor by actions or words show that we have taken offence, but for the sake of God continue to bear with and love our neighbour.

But Christ our Lord, besides His readiness to endure suffering and inconvenience caused by others, sacrificed also His own ease and rest, and deprived Himself at times of the necessaries of life, in His practice of the virtue of charity. On a certain occasion, as St. John relates, when journeying from Judæa into Galilee, Jesus passed through Samaria and came to the town of Sichar, where, being wearied with long travel and the mid-day heat, He sat down beside a well and held discourse with a woman of Samaria. As His most Sacred Body had been long without any sustenance, and the day was far spent, He felt much exhausted. His disciples, however, had gone to buy food, and on their return requested Him to eat. But our Lord declined to take the food which they had brought, because He expected the Samaritans to come to Him, and in order to devote Himself to a great work of charity, He disregarded all food or refreshment, however needful for His wearied Body.*

On another occasion, as we read in St. Mark, after preaching to the people, curing the sick, and performing other works of charity, at the dinner-hour our Lord entered, along with His disciples, a certain house for the purpose of taking food, but a multitude on perceiving Him flocked to the same house, and Christ, leaving the table, at once received the people and began to instruct them. St. Mark says expressly: "*The multitude cometh together again, so that they could not so much as eat bread.*"† This act of self-denial was often repeated, and the same Evangelist elsewhere narrates that when the Apostles had returned from their mission of preaching, and our Lord invited them

* St. John iv. 34.   † St. Mark iii. 20.

to refresh themselves in a place apart, "*there were many coming and going, and they had not so much as time to eat.*"* At this Theophylact cries out: "O happy crowd, which with so great frequency and earnestness pressed round our Lord to hear His doctrine, to witness His miracles, and lay hold on His salvation, that neither the Author Himself of salvation nor His disciples could find sufficient opportunity to take their food."†

True charity requires, and the example of Christ our Lord teaches us, that we must be prepared to sacrifice often some portion of our necessary rest, or sleep, of our food, or study, or temporal gains, and to submit to inconvenience and the want of many things that we need, so long as there is no danger of the serious loss of life or health, if we are to succour our neighbour in due time, and to console and rescue him when in corporal or spiritual difficulties. This personal sacrifice is especially incumbent on us when he needs our spiritual help in matters of instruction, or correction, or of the sacraments, or of sound advice, or when the emergency is so great that unless we act at once, however inconvenient, the fitting opportunity will be lost. St. Paul declares the quality of true charity to be such that "*it seeketh not its own,*"‡ that is to say, it does not place its own ease, or the advantages of honour, wealth, or pleasure, before the good of a neighbour, but seeks only the will and good pleasure of God.

The Apostle again exhorts this when he writes, Let all, in questions of religion and faith, "*be of one mind, having the same charity,*" loving the same good things, the same precepts of God, the same counsels: "*In humility, let each esteem others better than themselves;*" and let each one follow after these things, "*not considering those that are his own, but those that are other men's.*"§ Wherefore we are not to be always looking after our own interests, comforts, or tastes, but also after those of our neighbour; nay, we

---

* St. Mark vi. 31. † Theophyl. on St. Mark iii.
‡ 1 Cor. xiii. 5.   § Philipp. ii. 2, seq.

should even prefer their necessities before those things which are not so absolutely necessary for ourselves, and what conduces to the spiritual needs of their souls before our own temporal concerns; since this is the right order of holy charity. Nor was the Apostle content to express all this in words; he must also carry it out most perfectly in actions, following the example of Christ, and for our sakes drawing attention to his own example: "*As I also in all things,*" as far as possible, "*please all men, not seeking that which is profitable to myself,*" according to the flesh through temporal consolation, but seeking and procuring that which, as regards both soul and body, "*is profitable to many, that they may be saved.*"*

Let us now, however, inquire in what more particular way the Apostle gave up his own interest for the advantage of his neighbour. In a previous passage he writes: "*Whereas I was free unto all,*" being no man's servant or slave, I willingly "*made myself the servant of all, that I might gain all to Christ.*" And as a slave or servant dedicates himself entirely to the service of his master, so did I to that of all men: "*I became to the Jews as a Jew,*" accommodating myself to their customs in everything lawful; "*to them that are under the law*" of Moses, "*as if I were under the law,*" following certain legal observances, though, in truth, as regards the infidelity of those who would not believe in Christ, I was not a Jew, neither was I subject to nor bound by the law of Moses, which has already been brought to an end in the Gospel and the law of Christ, wherein I live. Yet in points that were lawful and not opposed to the Gospel, I conformed myself to them, that I might gain for Christ the souls of the Jews and of as many as "*were under the law.*" "*I became weak to the weak*" in faith and virtue, compassionating them, treating them kindly, and teaching them what it was easy for them to practice, "*that I might gain the weak*" for Heaven. Finally, "*I became all things to all men;*" I accommodated

* 1 Cor. x. 33.

myself to the conditions, dispositions, and tastes of all in things lawful, ceding my own rights, denying my own will, mortifying my own predilections, that, so far as I could, "*I might save all*," converting them to Christ.* In this way did St. Paul put in practice the virtue of charity, and we must copy his example, as He followed that of Christ. And however much we may have sacrificed our own conveniences in the cause of our neighbour's good, God will be well pleased, and we ourselves shall gather in the most precious fruit of spiritual and eternal life.

CHAPTER XXXIV.

Charity towards our neighbour must be so practised, that no act performed for him is opposed to the Divine will.

AMONGST the Divine cautions and directions to be strictly observed in all our works of charity one is, that in no single act of service rendered to a neighbour may we depart, even by a hair's breadth, from that which the law of God and the orders of superiors require. Some men are so blind as to think little of taking a false oath to save a neighbour from death, or of stealing money to give an alms to the poor. Others will in the cause of charity readily tell lies, spread false reports, and act in disobedience to their superiors. All such persons deceive themselves, because every work of true charity to our neighbour springs from the love of God, and the love of God obliges us to keep His Commandments in every respect, and to listen obediently to the directions of superiors. This law of action Christ has set before us with especial fulness; and though in each act of love which He performed He has given us example of this principle (in everything doing the will of His Eternal Father with the utmost perfection), yet is there one especial instance in which His example brings out the point before us most forcibly.

* 1 Cor. ix. 19, seq.

The Eternal Father sent His Son into the world, and ordained that He should take human flesh and appear visibly amongst men; and though the design of His coming was that He might save all of every nation on the earth, yet His visible appearance to hold intercourse with men, to preach, and to work miracles, was confined to the people of Israel, because to them alone had the promises been given. After all had been accomplished amongst this people that was requisite, the salvation of the Gospel was to be communicated to the other nations by means of His disciples. And this our Lord declared to the woman of Canaan: "*I was not sent but to the sheep that are lost of the house of Israel.*" * St. Paul also says that "*Christ Jesus was Minister of the Circumcision for the truth of God.*" † He came that by Himself, in the human nature which He assumed, He might fulfil the office and ministry of teaching, preaching, and performing miracles in the midst of that Jewish race which practised circumcision; and He did this to prove how true and faithful God is to all that He says and foretells, and to confirm the promises given to the fathers of old. And though Christ's love for all men was so boundless, as was also His wish to save all, and His desire to console and convert all by His power, His teaching, and His miracles; yet was He so faithful and exact in obeying the will and appointment of His Father, that when constantly passing through the cities and towns of Israel, and crossing from Judæa into Galilee and then back again, He never went beyond them, but the moment that He touched upon the boundary line, He turned and retraced His steps.

Of this the holy Evangelists take notice. St. Matthew observes that Jesus, passing with His disciples through Judæa, "*came to the quarters of Cæsarea Philippi,*" where He asked them: "*Whom do men say that the Son of Man is?*" ‡ And that He did not proceed any further, because He had reached at that point the limits of Judæa and the land

---

* St. Matt. xv. 24.   † Romans xv. 8.   ‡ St. Matt. xvi. 13.

of promise. Again, in crossing from Judæa into Galilee, "*Jesus retired into the coasts of Tyre and Sidon*,"* where He healed the daughter of the woman of Canaan ; but once more He checked His course, because Sidon was the boundary, nor would He enter those towns as belonging to the Gentiles. Moreover, He Who to the Jews was so liberal in healing all the sick and freeing all the possessed that were brought to Him, that He cured them almost without their asking, acted very differently with the woman of Canaan. At first, indeed, He would not even answer her, but went on His way ; it was only after her perseverance and importunity, that He at length rewarded the greatness of her faith. When likewise He was passing through Samaria, inhabited by Gentiles, which, as St. John reminds us, He would not have done had there been any other route from Judæa into Galilee, He avoided entering the city of Sichar until hard pressed to do so by the Samaritans of the place, even then He wrought no miracle there, but only preached to and instructed them.† When, during His mortal life, He sent His disciples out to teach and work miracles in the land of Israel, He added this prohibition : "*Go ye not into the way of the Gentiles, and into the cities of the Samaritans enter ye not.*"‡ Although after His Resurrection He bade them : "*Go ye into the whole world, and preach the Gospel to every creature.*" §

By this very marked succession of instances Christ instructed us that the acts of charity we do for our neighbour should be so carefully regulated as never to transgress the limits of the Divine law or of the obedience we owe to superiors. Thus, let no servant dare to give alms from his master's property, nor a son from that which belongs to his father, nor a religious subject from the goods of the monastery, and let no debtor omit to satisfy his creditor at the right time in order to give something in charity to the poor. So also a wife ought not, against

---

* St. Mark vii. 24.
† St. John iv. 4. ‡ St. Matt. x. 5. § St. Mark xvi. 15.

the command of her husband, to go out to attend the sick, nor a religious to preach or hear confessions without the leave of his superior. Nor may any one undertake a work of charity, of whatever importance, at the expense of even one lie, since it is more for a person's interest not to sin and thus break the commandment of God than to do a work of charity, which is a matter of counsel. The obligation to perform it ceases, nor can God desire it, if the doing it involves the smallest sin; for, as St. Paul decides: "*Evil may not be done, that thence there may come good.*" While, of those who declare the contrary, he says "*their damnation is just.*" *

The last confirmation of this teaching is that the Prophet Samuel, when in the name of God condemning the action of Saul, because in violation of the Divine command, he had "*spared the best of the flocks of sheep and of the herds*" for sacrifice to God, thus rebuked him: "*Obedience is better than sacrifices: and to hearken, rather than to offer the fat of rams.*" By which he signified to him that every act of obedience to a Divine or human commandment which is binding on us, is to be preferred before any voluntary work of religion or of mercy whatsoever. And this grave reason the Prophet further added: "*Because it is like the sin of witchcraft to rebel*" against the precept of a superior: "*and like the crime of idolatry, to refuse to obey.*"† As the soothsayer and the idolater worship the creature rather than the Creator by conceding to the creature that honour which they owe to the Creator alone, so he who is disobedient worships his own will and that of the devil, the instigator of his disobedience, instead of the will of God which justly demands his submission.

* Romans iii. 8. † 1 Kings xv. 9—23.

CHAPTER XXXV.

We ought in the spirit of charity to rejoice at the prosperity of our neighbour, as Christ teaches us by examples.

ONE of the first and principal exercises of fraternal charity is to take real interest and pleasure in our neighbour's welfare, in his virtuous and holy life, in his wisdom and prudence, in his ability, and in all his spiritual and corporal advantages for progress in virtue and in the salvation of his soul. St. Paul, speaking of charity, says that "*it rejoiceth with the truth,*"* that is it rejoiceth, not in the apparent and dangerous, but in the true and solid advantages of our neighbour, his belief in and love for and practice of what is truth, and in everything which may help him towards this end.

Our Lord gave us an example of this in His manner of dealing with His Apostles. For, whilst His disciples were performing miracles and casting out devils in His Name, some faithful persons amongst the people, although they did not accompany our Lord as His disciples, yet had considerable belief in His power, and began likewise to cast out devils through the invocation of His Name, God concurring with their act. The Apostles seeing this found fault, and imperiously prohibited those whom they observed from doing it, remarking that persons who were not disciples of Christ had no right to invoke His Name over the possessed, but should leave this office to them. One who had uttered this protest was St. John, and he, doubting whether he had done right, went and asked our Lord, saying: "*Master, we saw one,*" an Israelite, "*casting out devils in Thy Name, who followeth not us, and we forbad*

* 1 Cor. xiii. 6.

him. *But Jesus said: Do not forbid him, for he that is not against you is for you."* He who does not contradict your faith and doctrine, even though he does not follow Me by his external presence, is notwithstanding on your side, and acts with the desire to favour and assist you. For, all who have heard My teaching and witnessed My miracles are through them bound to believe in Me; there is no middle line, they must be either against Me, or for Me. If they do not accept My doctrine nor think well of Me, they are against Me, and are an offence to Me; but if they believe My word, and think and speak well of Me, they are for Me. And such are those of whom you speak, for in truth and in act they confess, praise, and magnify My Name, and are the cause that other men acknowledge its power.

By these words of instruction to His disciples Christ teaches us to acquiesce fully and rejoice in every good thing that we see in our neighbours, though perhaps they do not in any way associate with us, or may even keep themselves aloof; and whether it be one which affects their bodies or their souls, provided it is not opposed to the real benefit of their souls, but may conduce both to the service of God, and the good of the soul, it should give us real pleasure and delight, on account of the glory which may redound from it to God, and of the benefit which it brings to our neighbour.

To rejoice over the good of another, from which follows no diminution of either esteem or comfort to oneself, is an act of charity not at all difficult to accomplish. To rejoice, however, in the good fortune of a neighbour, which appears to us to affect our own reputation, and to lower and humble us before men, as when some favour or honour is granted to a companion and denied to ourselves, this cannot be accomplished so easily. Yet on this point also Christ has taught us how we ought to draw real consolation to ourselves from the good of our neigh-

* St. Mark ix. 37—40.

bour. St. Luke and St. Mark relate that when Jesus entered the house of the ruler of the synagogue to raise his daughter to life, He chose three out of the number of His twelve Apostles, namely, Peter, John, and James, to be the only disciples present at the miracle and able to bear witness to it, all the others being excluded without exception.* Again, when He ascended Mount Tabor to be transfigured, of all His Apostles and disciples He took only the same three; so that they alone looked upon the brightness of His bodily glory or could give testimony to that mystery.† The privilege conferred on those three Apostles was most marked and unusual, and, in the opinion of the world, would certainly lower the position of the other nine Apostles. Yet our Lord did not wish that these should be grieved or vexed at the particular favour granted to the three, but that they should, on the contrary, be contented and pleased that a favour denied to them should be granted to the three others.

Although St. Peter and St. John were both so intimate with and beloved by our Lord, yet after His Resurrection, passing by John along with all the others, He thrice charged St. Peter: "*Simon Peter, feed My lambs, feed My sheep.*"‡ He thus constituted him Shepherd and Bishop over the whole Church and over all the Apostles, and desired not that St. John should take this ill, but that both he and the rest should fully rejoice in the advancement of St. Peter. And this the Apostles did. For, though in their previous imperfect state they had shown a little irritation against some who wished to be more thought of than the rest, yet now they neither complained nor took the slightest offence at some being favoured more than others. And later on, after their souls had been inflamed with all the fervour of the charity of the Holy Ghost, they were filled with joy at the gifts and prerogatives which some received from God above others, they felt the greatest happiness in publishing them abroad,

* St. Mark v. 37.   † St. Matt. xvii. 1.   ‡ St. John xxi. 16.

because their whole desire was centred on this, that the will of God should be fulfilled by them. They held it to be their highest glory to please God, and as they saw that it was the will and good pleasure of God that in His Church there should be diversity of gifts, graces, and privileges, some greater and more eminent than others, and that it was God Himself Who thus distributed them, dividing according as He chose, they delighted themselves in those which each one had, feeling that in this way they could rejoice that the will of God was done, and could give greater pleasure to God Himself.

CHAPTER XXXVI.

Through the charity whereby we rejoice in the good of another envy is extinguished. What this vice is, and how it may be overcome.

THE practice of that charity which rejoices in the good of another destroys within us the most hurtful sin of envy, that would grieve over his good success. And since in recommending any particular virtue it is of much service to point out how the vice opposed to it can be avoided and overcome, we shall here briefly show in what way we ought to cleanse our hearts from envy through the exercise of fraternal charity.

Envy consists in the pain and sadness which some feel at the prosperity of a neighbour, because by it he has gained an advantage and superiority over them, and they deem themselves robbed thereby of the honour, importance, pre-eminence, or other advantage which they had obtained, or had sought, and set their hearts on obtaining. When any one is pained at the temporal gain of a neighbour on account of the injury which he expects or fears will arise from it, either to the person himself or to others; as, for instance, if he grieves at another's increase of wealth, being persuaded that he will abuse it, or spend it on sinful objects, or if he is distressed at another's appointment as judge or guardian, through fear of his misusing it to the injury of others, such anxiety is rather a virtue than a vice. Also, when a person is sad at another's success, not simply because his neighbour has that good, but because he himself has got only the same, or one like it, this is not envy, for his neighbour's success does not in itself displease him, but only in relation to that which he himself has, it is therefore the passion of vainglory and emulation. And in matters of spiritual good, if one grieve that he himself has not the patience, or prudence, or charity, or habit of prayer that others possess, his grief is not a fault, but a virtue.

When it is question of temporal good, and a man is distressed at not enjoying the wealth, distinctions, or gratifications that some neighbour has, if the kind of natural sorrow which he feels is caused by the want of some good necessary to his state of life, and is tempered by reason, it does not amount to a sin; but to be sad at not possessing goods that are superfluous is sinful, though it does not make a mortal sin so long as justice or charity remains uninjured. If, however, a man is aggrieved at his neighbour's good as an injury to himself, involving serious loss to his own honour and superior merits, which he is most desirous of maintaining unimpaired, then his feeling is unmistakably envy caused by his pride or excessive love of his own superior excellence. "As pride," says St. Augustine, "is a longing for distinction, he who seeks his own pre-eminence envies either his equals, because they are on a par with him, or his inferiors, lest they should come to rival him, or his superiors, because he cannot rise up to them. It is his pride, therefore, that makes him envious."*

If the advantage in another which saddens the envious

---

* St. Aug. lib. ii. *Super Gen.* cap xiii.

man is but of small moment as it affects his neighbour, for example, that another has a well-made coat, or is praised, that some person of rank has been more gracious to another than to him, his envy is then not mortal but venial. Or should his pain at another's good be only partial, not accompanied by a deliberate act of the will, or stopping short of a decided wish that his neighbour had never received so great a benefit, or might be deprived of it again by him if possible, then again the movement of envy constitutes only a venial sin. For, as Cajetan well observes, vexation is caused by that which is opposed to our will, and which we wish did not exist; when, therefore, our sadness has no wish in it that our neighbour should have never had, or should lose the good that vexes us, our sadness is not complete, and therefore our envy also is imperfect. The sadness indulged in with full and deliberate consent, and having for its cause a neighbour's undoubted good, such as his health, his means of life, an office of importance, his occupation, his learning, such sadness is a mortal sin, because it is opposed to charity, and is a fault of considerable gravity. Still further, should the good thus envied in a neighbour be a spiritual one, of virtue or grace, and cause displeasure at his having received from God so much virtue or grace, then does it indeed become a much more serious offence.

In truth, a sin so grievous as this is a rebellion against the Divine goodness. For as it is peculiar to what is good to communicate itself, and as God is infinite goodness, He communicates Himself in fullest measure to His creatures, and desires that all, especially men, should imitate Him in this, and should communicate to their neighbours the good which they have. But the envious man, by not wishing to communicate his good things, and by not desiring that God either should communicate them according to His own good pleasure to others, puts himself in direct opposition to the nature and will of God. He is therefore very far removed from God Himself, and estranged from His love and grace, according to the saying of the Wise Man: "*I will not go with consuming envy, for such a man shall not be partaker of*" Divine "*wisdom*,"* which is the gift of the Holy Ghost. As this sin renders a man on the one hand very unlike God, it on the other makes him very like the devil, to whom this vice specially belongs, since in it he began, in it he has persevered, and in it he will persevere most obstinately for all eternity. Through it he destroyed the world, and still contrives all the mischief that he can. Whence the Holy Scripture says: "*By the envy of the devil death came into the world; and they follow him that are of his side.*"† He envied our first parents that glory for which he saw they were created by God, and from which he himself had fallen, and he is followed by the sons of perdition, reprobated by God, who through sin have made themselves the sons of so vile a father and the servants of so iniquitous a master. St. Gregory thus writes, "By every sin, indeed, which man commits the venom of the old enemy is poured into man's heart, yet by this crime of envy the serpent stirs up all the malice within him, and vomits forth the vile infection of his malignant wickedness, that it may penetrate into man."‡

Another characteristic of this sin is that, as the devil tries to gratify his appetite, and draw some satisfaction from his malevolent acts, but tries in vain, nay, increases both his torment and his punishment; so an envious man strives in vain to gain some little importance and solace by grieving and lamenting over another's good, but adds to his own suffering thereby, because the bitterness, grief, and poignant anguish of his envy only rack his soul all the more, and feed on his body as well as his mind, according to the proverb of the Wise Man, "*Soundness of heart is the life of the flesh, but envy is the rottenness of the bones.*"§ As the heart which beats strongly and vigorously preserves the health of the body, and as the spiritual soundness of

---

* Wisdom vi. 25.   † Wisdom ii. 24, 25.
‡ St. Greg. *Mor.* lib. v. cap xxxi.   § Prov. xiv. 30.

the will through virtue and heavenly grace preserves the spiritual health of the soul; so, on the contrary, envy weakens and corrupts the bones of the soul, its virtues, that is, and powers, while it also enfeebles our corporal strength, and consumes our bodily health and life.

Such is, then, the sin of envy, such its gravity and malignity. Our duty is to fight against it by the holy exercise of fraternal charity, as we have already said, in rejoicing through God over all the good that comes to our neighbours; thus shall we overcome and destroy it. We live under many obligations to do this, for we are all fellow-members of one mystical body, the Church, and of one Head, Who is Christ. And as God has appointed that in the human body there should be many members, and that of these some should be more noble than others, He has also ordained that among each and all of them, the less and the more noble alike, the love and union should be of such a nature, that if one member suffers all the members suffer with it, so that the whole body becomes afflicted, and from each part of it the vital juices, the blood and other humours, flow together to help the part which suffers. Whence, if one member rejoices in its recovered health and strength, and receives natural relief from pain, all the other members share in its natural joy, acquiring new force and vigour, and being in a sounder state than before.

In which matter the Most High God, the Author both of nature and grace, has, on the authority of St. Paul, declared His will that, although of the faithful some are more exalted members of the Church, richer in corporal goods and spiritual gifts than others, yet that one and all should fully sympathize if but one member only suffer loss or damage, and should rejoice together as fully in the corporal and spiritual good of all.* And whilst we are thus joyful at their happiness we undoubtedly in a certain sense make his benefit our own, as St. Augustine said: 'Should a neighbour possess the grace of virginity, love him,

---

* 1 Cor. xii. 25.

and it is yours. You are possessed of greater patience, if he love you, it is his. He is gifted with watchfulness, provided you do not envy him, you profit by his study. You can, perhaps, fast more easily, if he loves you, he gains by your fast."* The meaning of the holy doctor is that a man by loving his neighbour and dwelling with pleasure on his virtue, participates in the merit of that virtue, and still more in the virtue and merit of Christ, of Whom he becomes a more perfect member, till in richer measure he attains the full merit of His heavenly glory.

CHAPTER XXXVII.

The means of acquiring the charity, by which we rejoice in our neighbour's good.

THE chief means that will render easy and pleasant to us the holy exercise of fraternal love is to transfer our desires from earthly to heavenly goods; to lay up treasure, not of empty and fleeting, but of solid, spiritual, and lasting riches; and to wish and strive after glory and excellence, as it is in truth and before God, not according to false appearances and the vain opinions of men. For since earthly goods are limited in value and of brief possession, the greater the number of those who enjoy them, the smaller will be each one's share. Hence arise envies, dissensions, quarrels, and wars between man and man, for the substance and position which one has, another is determined to deprive him of, and the importance and influence which one hopes for the other snatches from his grasp, and the distinction and privilege granted to one entail the discomfiture and disgrace of some other. And since in desiring and striving to gain earthly possessions men consult only their own will, it follows that the number of individual wills is equalled by the contentions, passions,

* S. Aug. lib. l. hom. xv.

injuries, and enmities, which stir up one against the other and prevent all real union or lasting friendship.

On the other hand, the spiritual goods of Heaven are immense and most varied, they exceed all price or limit, and the more widely they are spread amongst the servants of God, either on earth or in Heaven, the more rapidly do they grow and multiply, being a participation of the Divinity itself which makes them in a manner infinite, so that however plentifully God may distribute these gifts, there always remain many more still to give.

Besides this, these good things are endowed with the Divine faculty of enhancing the benefit, usefulness, and glory of all and every one of the just and of the blessed in proportion as their number increases; because there is a full communication of spiritual benefits between the saints of earth and those in Heaven. For in consideration of the gifts of grace which some possess, God grants particular favours to others; hence they who set their hearts on these possessions and are able to secure them have no feelings of envy against one another; the grace or glory of one can cause no displeasure in another, the rather do all greatly rejoice at the happiness of each individual, as each one rejoices in the happiness of the whole body. And more than this, since in desiring and seeking after spiritual blessings no one is guided by his own selfish wish, but by that appointment and good pleasure of God which are common to all, the pure-intentioned are free from dissension and strife, and enjoy complete union and peace.

The truth and efficiency of these means are exhibited to us in the person of St. John the Baptist, whose reputation and authority were so great amongst the people that they looked upon him as the Messias promised in the Law, and all followed and hung upon his words. In the height of his popularity, Christ began to manifest Himself and to work miracles, and, in proportion as the esteem in which our Lord was held increased, the public estimation of the great Baptist waned, till at length abandoning him the people followed the footsteps of Christ in large numbers and with the most intense admiration. The disciples of St. John on seeing this were filled with jealousy, and coming to him said: "*Rabbi, He that was with thee beyond the Jordan, to Whom thou gavest testimony, behold He baptiseth,*" through His disciples, "*and all men come to Him.*"* In this difficulty a man whose heart was set upon earthly honour and reputation would have done his best, in his jealousy and indignation, to strip our Lord of His influence with the people. But in the depth of his humility, St. John, whose whole heart was set upon God and the fulfilment of His most holy will, felt only the keenest joy at the news of Christ's increasing repute, and of his own decreasing favour with the people; for he knew this to be the Divine will and design, and that it most befitted the Divine glory; this therefore he himself ardently desired.

And this joy of his heart, together with its cause, St. John openly expressed: "*A man cannot receive anything, unless it be given him from Heaven.*" As though he had said, a man cannot acquire or retain any good, any dignity or authority, unless it is bestowed on him by God, either immediately or through His creatures; and thus I neither possess now, nor have I possessed hitherto, more influence or honour with men than God has been pleased to give me; with this am I most content, nor would I wish more, because I simply desire that in everything His will may be done. That which it belonged to me to desire through all my life, the coming, namely, of this Lord, and His manifestation and recognition amongst men through my testimony, this is now fulfilled; wherefore, "*it behoveth that He should increase,*" in authority, and esteem, and acceptance before men, in order that He may be acknowledged and received as the true Christ and Saviour of the world. But it behoves that I decrease in the high opinion of men, that all may see that I am not the Messias, but only His servant and forerunner. St. John's reason

* St. John iii. 26.

therefore for rejoicing instead of sorrowing at the diminution of his own dignity and authority was that in everything he desired and sought the will and glory of God.

And it was on account of this his charity and humility that, although he suffered for a brief space the decrease of his earthly glory, yet that day of humiliation being passed, he received even on earth from the lips of Christ Himself the honour of the highest praise and acknowledgment of sanctity that was ever accorded to the saints of God. And it was God's own act that published his praise throughout the world by means of the inspired writing of Evangelist and Apostle, that all the faithful from the commencement of the Church should honour him, and hold him in highest veneration in every age until the world's end, and that in Heaven he should be placed amongst the highest Seraphim in supreme glory.

After this manner we too, seeking in all things God's will and glory, should not grieve at the little esteem that men may have of us, or at their positive contempt, or at the withdrawal of their former respect from us, but, on the contrary, be glad thereat, as being in accordance with the will and appointment of God; for, instead of losing, we the more increase that spiritual and heavenly gain in which our heart is truly fixed. And we should rejoice in our neighbour's good, for because of such humility and charity we shall be highly esteemed of God, and of His angels and saints, we shall on earth be numbered amongst the sons of God and be honoured by the gifts of His grace, and in Heaven we shall enjoy the riches of His glory.

CHAPTER XXXVIII.

How our Lord through this means of desiring, not earthly, but heavenly goods, cured the tendency of His disciples to envy. His wish that all should use the same remedy against this vice.

BY the remedy which we have now explained, Christ cured those movements to envy which infected the hearts of the Apostles, while as yet imperfect in virtue and unskilled in the spiritual life. When the ten Apostles heard the two brothers, St. John and St. James, venturing to petition our Lord that He would assign them the highest places in His Kingdom, and saw that their request was rejected, they were stirred with indignation against their fellow-Apostles, and a certain feeling of emulation and envy began to burn within their breasts at the desire of these two brothers to be above them. Our Lord at once called them aside that He might remove this feeling from their hearts and cure their disease. "*Jesus called them to Him and said, You know that the princes of the Gentiles lord it over them,*" that amongst Gentiles who know neither the true God nor His glory, but seek earthly glory, all princes, rulers, and masters domineer over their subjects, and do with them much as they like, and in their government they consult, not the peace and benefit of their subjects, but the increase of their own authority, dignity, and advantage. "*And they that are the greater, exercise power upon them,*" recklessly and imperiously requiring them to do whatever pleases themselves, and binding them to this without any regard for truth or justice, but simply for their own cupidity and gratification. "*It shall not be so among you, but whosoever will be the greater among you, let him be your minister. And* *he that will be first among you, shall be your servant.*"* His meaning evidently is that those who should be hereafter placed in charge as Superiors, were to devote themselves to the real good, to the spiritual health and necessities of their subjects, as the ministers and servants of men of noble rank devote themselves entirely to the service of their masters. There was therefore no occasion for their desiring and aiming after power, or honour, or worldly distinction; but they ought to seek the good of those placed under them, and labour and spend themselves for them, as though they were their servants.

After our Lord had thus warned His disciples against following the false principles and practice of the Gentiles, He at once placed a safe guide before them, "*Even as the Son of Man is not come to be ministered unto, but to minister, and to give His life a redemption for many.*" I, the true Son of God, and Myself truly God, came into the world and was made Man, holding visible intercourse with men; and came, not that men should in this world serve Me, but that I might serve them. Wherefore from My infancy I served My most holy Mother, and served her spouse, St. Joseph, assisting him in his trade of carpenter up to nearly the thirtieth year of My age. Again, after I had manifested Myself to Israel, I ministered to the sick in curing their diseases, and to the ignorant in teaching them heavenly doctrine, to the multitudes by feeding them in the wilderness, to My disciples by breaking bread for them, and with My own hands helping them to what was on the table. Besides which I especially came to minister to all men, giving My life and My Blood as an all-sufficient ransom for the redemption of the world, and an effectual purchase-money for many, namely, for the elect. In this way have I laboured and suffered for the good and for the healing of all men, as though I were the servant of all; and you, my disciples, ought in all this to imitate Me and copy My example, doing that which I have done, and spending

* St. Matt. xx. 24—27.

yourselves for the good and benefit of each one amongst you, as I have spent Myself.

By this instruction Christ removed the early germs of envy and pride from the hearts of His disciples, and laid before us that effectual remedy which each one should apply for the cure of this vice; that we should love, desire, and actively seek not office, or honour, or earthly advantages, as men of the world do, but those true spiritual and heavenly gifts, and that spiritual and temporal good which help to the salvation both of our own souls and theirs. O most pure teaching of Christ, shining out clearer and brighter than the sun itself! O doctrine so truly heavenly, proceeding from the Heart of God, which He our Lord hath announced to the world: *"For this cause was I born, and for this came I into the world, that I should give testimony to the truth."**

Nor did Christ heal His disciples alone from this sin of envy, but (what is more wonderful) by a word He touched the heart of a Gentile woman of Canaan, and cured her of a vice so deadly and so powerful among unbelievers. When our Lord had "*retired into the coasts of Tyre and Sidon, behold a woman of Canaan came out to Him saying, Have mercy on me, O Lord, my daughter is grievously troubled by a devil.*"† When our Lord at first refused to answer her, she continued following and entreating Him, till at last she came near to Him, "*and adored Him, saying, Lord, help me. Who, answering, said, It is not good to take the bread of the children and to cast it to the dogs,*" thus giving the name of bread to His doctrine, miracles, and all other means ordained for the salvation of souls, as being the spiritual food of souls, and thus, also, calling the Jews by the title of sons, as the people of God who possessed His faith and religion, amongst whom were just men and true sons of God, and finally applying to the Gentiles the epithet of dogs, because of the cruelties practised by them in the worship of their false gods.

* St. John xviii. 37. † St. Matt. xv. 22.

Our Lord spoke thus harshly to the woman to humble her, and make her acknowledge herself unworthy to obtain her petition, as belonging to a generation and Gentile sect not professing the true God. He wished her moreover to understand that the Jews justly held the preference, inasmuch as He came to work these miracles of healing, and of casting out devils, not for the Gentiles but for the chosen people. The woman received this lesson of humility with all meekness, taking no offence at being called a dog, making no complaint at the great favours and rich benefits reserved by Christ for the Jews, nor envious of their being so highly honoured as to be called the sons of God. So far from this, she certainly acknowledged it to be well done, yet so that even then her petition might be heard; for, although she was too unworthy to deserve it, it well became the goodness of so great a Lord to grant His favour even to the unworthy. And all this her words implied: "*Yea, Lord, for the whelps also eat of the crumbs that fall from the tables of their masters;*" I do not indeed deny, O Lord, that the Jews are sons, and we but dogs; that they as being sons sit at the table of God the Father, Who possesses all things, and eat the most precious food of His teaching, His miracles, His sacraments and heavenly gifts; still to me as a dog it is not denied to eat of the crumbs which fall from the Master's table. That miracle which I stand in so great need of is but a crumb compared with those rich and abundant favours in which the Jews rejoice, this crumb alone I ask, and with it shall I be content, and it wholly befits the liberality of so rich a Father that this crumb should be granted to me.

Such then is the heavenly medicine offered to us for purging our souls from every trace of this disease of envy, that we turn aside from the empty advantages of the world and with our whole hearts seek those real benefits which sanctify and rejoice our souls, desiring temporal things only in so far as they help us to attain that end. With this spirit we shall gladly accept humiliations coming from

God, and injuries and insults inflicted by men, as means helping to a securer possession of the eternal good which we desire. To this the Apostle exhorts us: "*Let us not be made desirous of vainglory, provoking one another,*" with words and actions that breed strife and contention; "*envying one another,*" in our grief at another's good.* These vices are fed by vainglory; destroy that passion, and these sins die out. Again, elsewhere: "*Let nothing be done through contention,*" through obstinate quarrelling to gain one's end and overthrow another, "*neither by vainglory,*" hoping to gain applause and influence amongst men, "*but in humility,*" thinking only of oneself, "*let each esteem others better than themselves,*" abler or more worthy; "*not considering the things that are his own,*" unless indeed those sins that should make him despise himself and regard himself as inferior to all, "*but considering those that are other men's,*" gifts bestowed on them by God, in that they are His image, that they possess Christ through grace, that they profess His faith and belong to His Church, and are guarded by His angels.† For, as each one is judge over himself, and not over his neighbour, he ought to humble, correct, and punish himself for his sins, but to love and highly esteem his neighbour on account of all the good gifts which he has received from God.

CHAPTER XXXIX.

The order according to which we should regulate our love of our neighbour. The extent and reasons for our love even of bad men.

IT is true, as we have before said, that the virtue of charity requires us to love all men, the good and the bad, sinners as well as just men; we must, however, regulate our love, extending more of it to the good and just than to the bad and wicked. Sinners are to be loved on the ground that

* Galat. v. 26.   † Philipp. ii. 3, 4.

they are our neighbours, capable of and created for happiness; also because Christ loved them, and through that love gave His life for them, and now calls and sanctifies them, and, if they turn to obey Him, will make them happy. Another reason for loving them is, that this same Lord desires and commands us to love them, and takes delight in our doing so; while to those who thus love them He promises an eternal reward, but threatens never-ending punishment to those who hate them.

In our love of bad men this distinction, however, must be observed: we are to love them according to that nature which in each one is of or from God, not according to that sin in them which is of man, and which we are bound to hate. We should love them as creatures of God, made after His image, and we should desire and strive to procure for them every good that is of use either to body or soul, but do our best to purify their souls of all guilt and sin. In this way, to hate them as sinners is to love them, for it implies the desire to deliver them out of sin through the help of God's grace. As St. Augustine explains, "No sinner, in so far as he is a sinner, is worthy of our love; but every sinner, in so far as he is a man, is to be loved for the sake of God."* And in another place he writes: "He who is the servant of God should have a perfect and holy hatred of sinners, yet so as neither to hate the man himself because of his sin, nor to love the sin because of the man who is guilty of it; but so as to hate the sin while he loves the man."†

Let us inquire briefly how we are to detect the principle on which we really act. It is shown by our compassionating the sinner, grieving over his sin, and desiring the safety of his soul and all the temporal good for him that can help towards his salvation; and if we desire that God, or one having authority over him, should visit him with some punishment, we do this only in the hope of his correcting

---

* St. Augustine, lib. i. *De Doct. Christ.* cap. xxvii.
† Idem, *De Civit. Dei*, lib. xiv. cap. vi.

and amending himself, and of preventing his injuring others. Punishment that is not necessary, or that is useless to this end, should not be desired by us, but we should rather leave it in God's hands to correct him in the way that most pleases God. Thus St. Gregory: "True justice and sanctity feels compassion for a neighbour when in a state of sin; false sanctity conceives great indignation against him. Though even good men are indignant with sinners, as sinners, yet that zeal which is enkindled by pride, is of a very different stamp from the zeal of holy correction," which aims at amending the sinner and deterring others. It is not, then, in hatred, but in love that they "stir up a persecution against the wicked, for though externally and as matter of discipline they find very heavy fault with them, yet privately charity makes them gentle towards them."* St. Gregory well distinguishes a proper indignation from that which is false and inconsistent, in that the latter wishes evil to the man who has sinned for his injury, because he hates him, whereas the former wishes him to be punished for his good, because he loves him.

Certain philosophers, and amongst them Aristotle, considered it lawful, nay, an act of virtue, to grieve over the temporal good of a bad man, his health, for instance, life, riches, honour, on the plea that the sinner is unworthy of such benefits as these, and that it is a pity he should have them. But such an opinion is opposed to the Divine law and to right reason. Were this displeasure caused by the injury such success would have on the sinner himself, and on others through him, then it would not be wrong, because it would be directed to the good of our neighbour, and would spring from charity. But displeasure merely at his possessing what he does not deserve is bad, and is condemned in Scripture: it would be even a great sin if the good in question were of a decided value. The bad man, indeed, may not deserve it, but yet God in His infinite goodness has willed to

* St. Augustine, Hom. xxxiv. *In Evang.*

bestow benefits upon the unworthy as upon all men without exception, seeing that all men were, through sin, undeserving of any good, and deserved only eternal death: it is not therefore for our merits' sake that God has conferred His benefits on us. In truth, God manifests His infinite goodness precisely in communicating Himself and in doing good to all, and very especially does He do so in granting His benefits to sinners unworthy of any one good thing.

Besides this manifestation of His goodness, God has other objects in view, most worthy of Himself, for in the temporal advantages which He grants to the wicked He recompenses them for certain morally good actions which they may have done, though justice does not strictly bind Him to this; He by the same means often brings them to the knowledge of their sinfulness and excites them to repentance. By the favours which He shows to the bad He inspires great hope in the good men that He will take still more care of them in giving them those spiritual favours for which they earnestly pray to Him, since He is so very liberal in bestowing temporal gifts on sinful men who prize them most. Now, seeing that this dispensation of God's providence is so excellent, and is so worthy of God, for a man to grieve over the benefits which God, either directly from Himself, or through His creatures, grants to the sinner, and to wish that he should be deprived of them, is an act of injustice against both God and his neighbour. This fault was condemned by Christ in His Gospel, when, under the figure of a householder, He rebuked those labourers who complained that He had paid their fellow-workmen above their deserts. "*Is thy eye evil because I am good?*"* In other words, from My goodness and liberality in paying at a higher rate than I am bound or have promised, dost thou take occasion to judge rashly and murmur against that which you ought to approve of and praise?

Let us then, rejecting those principles of the world

* St. Matt. xx. 15.

which only deceive it, and following rather the teaching brought down from Heaven to us by Christ, love our neighbours truly from our hearts, even though they be wicked and sinful, and let us in their regard obey the law of true charity, wishing them and extending to them every necessary good, grieving over their faults, and rejoicing in whatever spiritual and temporal benefit they have; for thus shall we conform ourselves to the will of their Lord and Heavenly Father, " *Who*," in the words of His only-begotten Son Jesus Christ, "*maketh His sun to rise upon the good and bad, and raineth upon the just and the unjust.*"*

CHAPTER XL.

In what degree the good are to be more loved by us than the bad.

IF sinners are to be beloved by us as we have described, for the sake of God, how much more ought the just and holy to obtain our love? Although according to the substance of the good which we desire for our neighbours, we are bound to love all men equally, wishing that all should be saved and attain the blessed sight and possession of God in Heaven; yet in respect of the degree of affection wherewith we desire this for them, and the result which our help is likely to bring about; in respect also of the greater perfection in which this infinite good is possessed through grace here on earth, and fully entered upon in the glory of Heaven, we love, and we ought to love one neighbour more than another.

Hence, all other points being equal, the good are more to be beloved by us than the bad; in the first place, because the good are more closely united to God, are more like Him, more fully participate in Him, and are more beloved by Him. And since we are bound to love sinners

* St. Matt. v. 45.

because they share in our common human nature, and in a limited love from God, moving Him to communicate to them natural and temporal benefits and good inspirations, much more ought we to love the just on account of the grace dwelling in them, of the glory waiting for them, and of that absolute and wholly perfect love which God bears to them, communicating to them His supernatural gifts of grace, and confirming them with the pledge and right to eternal beatitude, into which He will in due time admit them. St. Ambrose exclaims: "More, most certainly, should we love those neighbours, in whose company we expect and hope to dwell for ever, than those with whom we spend this life only." *

In the second place, we are bound to love those more whose lives are more productive of good to the whole Church and to the particular members of it; and the benefits which redound to all the faithful from the virtues and companionship of the good are indeed many and great, since by their exterior manner, their words, and their whole example they edify us, and inflame our hearts with the love of God and of all virtue. As St. Gregory says, he who for his own spiritual profit "seeks the company of some holy man, does through a careful observation of his life, through listening to his holy conversation, through the example of his great works, dispel from his own heart the deep shadows of his past sins, and becomes inflamed with a desire for heavenly light and with the love of virtue."† St. Isidore expresses this more briefly: "If he be admitted to share in his conversation, he will share also in his virtue." ‡ Also through the prayers of good men, and through the union and intercourse which we naturally hold with them as belonging to the same faith, religious order, city, or house, we are freed from many evils, misfortunes, and Divine visitations which would befall us but for their presence, as God through the mouth

* St. Amb. lib. i. *De Officio*, cap. vii.
† St.Greg. Hom. v. *In Ezech.*   ‡ St. Isid. lib. ii. *Synn.* cap. viii.

of Jeremias and Ezechiel tells us, and as He Himself intimated to Abraham when He promised that, could even ten men be found in Sodom, He would arrest the punishment of fire from Heaven, by which He was about to destroy the city and all its inhabitants, on account of their abominable sins.* Nor are we only preserved from evils by our union and companionship with good men, God also on account of it communicates to us innumerable spiritual and temporal blessings; as is likewise evident from Scripture, for instance, where we are told that "*the Lord blessed the house of Putiphar, an Egyptian, and chief captain of Pharao's army, for Joseph's sake,*" who being a servant of the true God was also a member of the Egyptian's household; and that God "*multiplied all his substance, both at home and in the fields.*"† And Laban confesses his own similar experience to Jacob, while he lodged that servant of God in his house: "*I have learned by experience, that God hath blessed me for thy sake.*" ‡

Now if God, in consideration of His faithful servants, bestows thus liberally on those who do not profess faith in Him such temporal benefits as they desire, and their want of faith does not debar them from receiving, it is clear that, for the sake of those same good men, God will far more readily communicate to members of His true Church, and especially to its faithful members the fullest measure of His Divine and spiritual gifts, such as they truly desire, aim after, and highly prize.

For these reasons, though we owe to all men the love of charity, we owe a much fuller share of it to good men, than to bad, as Christ taught us by His own example. Our Lord loved all men in the world, the good and the bad, for all of whom He offered up His life; but during His mortal life on earth, in that most holy will by which He loved all men on account of the love which He saw the Father bore towards them from all eternity, He had

---

* Jerem. v. 1; Ezech. xxii. 30; Gen. xviii. 32.
† Genesis xxxix. 5.   ‡ Genesis xxx. 27.

a greater love for the children of Israel, amongst whom He was born and grew up, than He had for other nations, because the Jews formed the body of the faithful and professed the true religion, and many members of the race were holy men. Amongst His own people He felt a greater and a special love for His own Apostles and disciples who followed and accompanied Him, seeing that these were still more holy and more faithful to the Divine call. To these, therefore, as being more beloved than the rest, He gave both in act and word greater marks and evidences of His love; saying to them for example: "*I have called you*" special "*friends,*" and as such have treated you "*because all things whatsoever I have heard of My Father, I have made known to you.*"* Of Jews who were neither Apostles nor disciples, He had a greater and particular love for Lazarus, and his sisters Mary and Martha, as St. John testifies. The sisters of Lazarus "*therefore sent to Jesus, saying: Lord, behold, he whom Thou lovest is sick. . . . Now Jesus loved Martha, and her sister Mary, and Lazarus.*" † By which terms the Evangelist wished to express a love marked by especial signs of friendship.

That which moved our Lord to love these persons more than His other followers was that He saw in them a more perfect virtue, love, and obedience than in any others. Thus Simon de Cassia plainly states: "Jesus loved Martha and Mary her sister and Lazarus, not because they were of high rank, nor because they were rich, but because He knew their love towards Himself, and it should be the constant and chief effort of every one to love Jesus Christ, and to be beloved by Him." ‡ And as Christ loved them more than others because they were more holy, for the same reason he treated them with greater familiarity, visiting them, being very kind to them, and giving them especial help in any difficulty; he turned aside also to

---

* St. John xv. 15.
† St. John xi. 3, 5.   ‡ Simon de Cass. lib. v. cap. xv.

dwell in their house, and partook of food there along with His disciples. St. Chrysostom writes, "Christ went to Bethany, and remained in the house of Martha and Mary, because it is the wont of holy men not to visit in the houses of those who lay many dishes before them, but of those who are richer in virtue and holiness of life."* By these and other examples Christ teaches us that it is most just, and most in accordance with His will, that good and holy men should be loved rather than those who are the reverse, and that they should receive a fuller share of our love.

CHAPTER XLI.
Other reasons why the good should be loved by us rather than the bad.

CHRIST has given us other reasons for especially loving good men, which are deserving of our consideration. The first of them is that holy men have done more good to the souls of those who have loved them, and proved their love to them by deeds. Our Lord taught this when He said, "*Make unto you friends of the mammon of iniquity,*" that is, of riches which are ordinarily the occasion of many sins, "*that when you shall fail they may receive you into everlasting dwellings.*"† By these friends may indeed be meant the poor to whom alms are given, since in return for the charity extended to them, and the help bestowed in a true spirit of charity, the reward is promised of being received by Christ and His angels and saints into heavenly habitations. But more properly speaking their friends are just men who, renouncing everything for the sake of Christ, have made themselves poor, and are straitened in temporal circumstances. The words of Scripture are more truly verified in them, because by their merits and prayers they receive into the heavenly dwellings those who have mani-

* St. Chrysost. hom lxvii. *In Matt.* xxi.   † St. Luke xvi. 9.

fested their love and their charity towards them, and have assisted them in their necessities. For through their holy lives and the efficacy of their prayers they render God propitious and merciful to those that helped them, and they obtain from His goodness that He should grant them the favours and graces needful to raise them to the most glorious dwellings of eternal happiness. Hence, although every work of charity done for any neighbour is most useful, and has its reward, yet that which is done for the holy and perfect is far more useful, and will obtain a more excellent reward.

St. Augustine explains the words in this sense, "Who are they that shall enter the everlasting dwellings, if they be not the saints of God? And who are they that shall be received by them into the everlasting dwellings, but they who have helped their needs, and have gladly ministered to them in all that they required?" The saints who shall receive into Heaven those that before succoured them, "are the least of the servants of Christ, who have abandoned everything for Christ, and have followed Him in the way of perfection, and whatever they had they distributed it to the poor, that they might be free to serve God without any worldly hindrance, and thus, liberated from earthly burdens (and the troublesome cares of secular life), they rise up towards Heaven as though on wings."*

Another proof of this great fruit of charity was given by our Lord to His disciples when He said, "*He that receiveth you,*" by being kind to you and supplying your temporal wants, "*receiveth Me; and he that receiveth Me, receiveth,*" by the same act, "*Him that sent Me. He that receiveth a prophet,*" a preacher and minister of My Gospel, "*in the name of a prophet,*" because he is My minister, "*shall receive the reward of a prophet: and he that receiveth a just man in the name of a just man,*" as being a faithful servant of God, "*shall receive the reward of a just man.*"†
He spoke differently of the humble, when He said, "*Who-*

* St. Aug. *De Verb. Dom.* Serm. xxxv. † St. Matt. x. 40, 41.

soever shall receive one such child as this in My name receiveth Me. And whosoever shall receive Me, receiveth not Me" alone, but at the same time, "*Him that sent Me.*"* By which words Christ indicates this mystery to us, that the charity and fraternal love which are exercised in acts coming from the heart for the benefit of good men, and more particularly for the ministers of His Gospel, who are busy in the salvation of souls, are more highly pleasing to God, produce more effect for the benefit of others, and exercise a singular influence with Him in obtaining a richer reward from His goodness. In this lies the especial "*reward of a prophet,*" and the especial "*reward of a just man.*" In this way Christ also shows how highly He esteems and loves His holy and faithful ministers, seeing that He not only confers favours on them and very greatly rewards their virtue, but for their sakes bears a peculiar love to those who assist them, and who are loved by them in turn, bestows higher benefits on them, and makes them worthy to receive a fuller reward in return for kindnesses done to His ministers.

There is yet another reason for which God gives this especial reward. When any servant of God either performs an act of kindness, or assists from his temporal means, or himself takes a part with the just man and minister of Christ in good works, and in bringing souls to God, in instructing others, in obtaining for them the sacraments, or in any other works of spiritual mercy, he participates in the fruits of the good work done, and cooperates in the holy ministry for souls, and therefore will justly receive from God a reward similar to that which is granted to the just man and to the minister of God, whom he has helped by his means or by his own personal service. For though the just man may possess more of this world's goods, yet he enjoys the holy liberty of preaching the truth, of defending virtue, and another who maintains and assists him, becomes a sharer in his holiness and sanctity, and will

---

* St. Mark ix. 36.

receive a reward along with him. And that teacher or minister of the Gospel in whom the Holy Spirit dwells must have bodily nourishment to strengthen him for his work, and without which he cannot work; another, therefore, who supplies him with this, supplies him with strength to preach and fulfil all the other holy offices of his ministry, for this reason he will receive a reward along with the minister of Christ.

CHAPTER XLII.

The reasons which should direct us in loving some neighbours more than others.

WE have considered the order which we should follow in loving sinners, and men of holiness of life, and the ministers of Christ, let us now consider the order in which charity is to be practised towards our different neighbours. In regard of our parents, of our brothers and sisters, of our relations, and of all others united with us by some particular bond of connection or affinity, or of fellow-membership in the same state, city, or household, we owe greater love, and a more perfect performance of works of charity, than we do towards others who have not these claims upon us. The explanation of this is, that love is founded in some mutual communication and union between persons, and the closer this union is, so much the greater should the love be. Besides, grace perfects instead of destroying nature, and we see that all men have this natural inclination to love those who stand in a nearer relation to them. Nor is this a tendency introduced by sin, but one founded on right reason; so that had men persevered in that state of pure and healthy nature which God at first gave them, they would still have had this inclination. Wherefore grace does not destroy, but only restrains and directs it, that it run not to extreme, and that it may propose God as its true end. St. Augustine writes:

L

"Since you cannot do good to every one, you must first select those who by reason of place or time, or some other circumstance, are by a kind of providence more particularly connected with you."* And the Apostle confirms the same principle: "*But if any man have not care of his own, and especially of those of his house, he hath denied the faith, and is worse than an infidel.*"† This care of which the Apostle speaks is to be taken as embracing proper instruction as regards the soul, and for the body the providing of all things necessary, and this with especial reference to servants and members of the same family, towards whom the obligation is greatest. The faith which he hath denied is that duty to God and to all dependent on him to which the natural law binds him; such a man is worse than an infidel, because many of these in obedience to their natural reason attend to this duty. And since the obligation of helping those brought into closer connection with us is the stronger, for the external act proceeds from the interior affection, it follows that those ought to have the preference before strangers. This principle holds good as long as relatives and neighbours are equal in other respects to the rest of our neighbours; if however there be any inequality, this rule is not to be followed in every case. For, if the necessity of a relation or neighbour is not very grievous, and he can without much injury to himself live on what he has, while the need of some stranger is so urgent that he is wanting in what is necessary for the barest existence, then is the stranger to be assisted before the other. And in proportion as this person, more remotely connected with us, possesses greater dignity, and is of greater utility to the state or to the spiritual good of souls, whilst the necessities of those nearer to us are not more grievous, well-ordered charity demands that succour should be given to this person first, since the public good takes precedence of the private, as is especially seen in the case of works of mercy.

* St. Aug. lib. i. *De Doct. Christ.* cap. xxviii.   † 1 Tim. v. 8.

There is another point we must attend to here. If a distantly-connected neighbour be of holy life and great virtue, and those nearer to us are bad, or at all events inferior to him in virtue, then must we so observe charity that the good are more loved by us, more esteemed, and receive more solid benefit, by our desiring higher glory for them than for near neighbours whose virtue is much inferior. We should wish also to see Divine justice preserved, which requires that the greater glory should be bestowed on him who merits more, nor ought we to wish that God should grant to a neighbour whose merit is so much less, a degree of glory which in his present disposition he does not deserve. This, however, charity does not forbid our desiring, namely, that God may make a sinful neighbour as good as, nay, better than any other saint on the earth, and that for this end He may impart to him higher aids and graces than to others, by help of which he can merit and obtain higher glory. It is, moreover, lawful for us, with a view to those spiritual goods for the sake of which we love our neighbours, to bear them a more intense and ardent affection of charity, according to the dispositions which we see in them. For, in addition to the general friendship of charity and grace, there is a natural and human friendship which we can direct towards the same end of charity, by desiring for them still more of the spiritual benefits of grace and glory, as also of temporal benefits helping them forward to that end.

In this mode of showing charity to those most nearly connected with us, Christ has not left us without example. He was born in Bethlehem, and to all the inhabitants and near neighbours of that time, He, in His wondrous charity, gave advantages above all other Jews of possessing most glorious martyrs in their "children of two years old and under," on whom He bestowed in Heaven the brightest crowns of martyrdom, and raised them to higher glory than was ever attained before by infants dying in Divine grace since the beginning of the world. That crown of martyrdom, which by a singular grace and privilege is usually bestowed only on saints after many years of mature life spent in constant labours and prayer, was here granted to infants who had neither laboured, nor merited, nor had even attained the use of reason. And at the same time that on these infants He conferred the benefit of so extraordinary a charity, He bestowed a like favour upon their parents, making them the fathers and mothers of martyred children, whom He gave again to them as their guardians and advocates with God. By this most glorious martyrdom of so many infants, He cast an incredible lustre over Bethlehem and all its neighbourhood.

Christ dwelt, for the most part, in lower Galilee, inhabited by the tribe of Zabulon, near to the lake of Genesareth, along with St. Joseph and the Blessed Virgin, from His return out of Egypt till His manifestation to Israel, whence He was called by men the Galilæan.* And since this was the humblest and most despised province of Judæa, as the Pharisees remarked to Nicodemus, "*Search the Scriptures, and see that out of Galilee a prophet riseth not,*"† our Lord, when about to appoint His Apostles, who were to be the princes and foundation stones of His Church, teachers of the whole world, and universal judges over the twelve tribes of Israel, and over every nation on the earth, as well as the highest courtiers of His Kingdom in Heaven, He chose them, too, out of this province of Galilee, and from beside this lake of Genesareth, while, in the midst of their nets and fishing boats, they were following the humble trade of fishermen. And, though not all were fishers, yet all were born in Galilee; so that when the Jewish strangers heard them, after the descent of the Holy Ghost, speaking in their different tongues, they exclaimed with wonder, "*Behold, are not all these that speak Galilæans? And how have we heard every man our own tongue wherein we were born?*"‡ Thus did Christ

---

* St. Matt. xxvi. 69.   † St. John vii. 52.
‡ Acts ii. 7, 8.

greatly ennoble, magnify, and exalt to Heaven the province in which He dwelt.

Within the province of this very Galilee, the least of all its towns, was Nazareth, in which our Lord was conceived and grew up till He was about thirty years old.* After His fast in the desert, when He went forth to make Himself known in Israel, He began to preach in the town of Nazareth; and He entered the synagogue, and, taking up the book, read that prophecy in Isaias which spoke concerning Himself, and He declared before them all that the prophecy was now fulfilled in Himself. Thus did He begin His public teaching by the exercise of charity to His fellow-citizens and the dwellers in His own country, instructing them, illuminating them, opening out Divine mysteries to them, and leading them along the way of life. And at the same time He taught to us the true order of charity, how, while the necessities of all were equal, those more nearly connected with Him were to be preferred to others, as Theophylact remarks—"Our Lord, when about to manifest Himself to Israel, showed Himself first to the people of Nazareth amongst whom He lived, that He might teach us that we ought to do good first of all to those nearest us, and most connected with us, and after that extend our charity to all other neighbours."†

CHAPTER XLIII.

Although some persons ought to be loved above others, yet in all external intercourse marks of censure and offence must be carefully avoided.

IN the order of our charity, though the good ought to be more loved than the wicked, and the holier more than the less holy, and those nearly connected with us more than those who are strangers, yet as this love is to be exercised for the sake of God, so must it be moderated and regulated

* St. Luke iv. 16.   † Theophyl. *In Luc.* iv.

according to His will and good pleasure, with a view to that which most befits His glory and the good of souls. Hence, if a person lives much in society, or has to deal with many in general conversation and intercourse, on account of his office or profession, he is not justified if, on the ground of one being better than another, or brought into closer relationship with him, he shows him such marks of his private esteem as will offend others, or be an occasion to them of sin. All parents, superiors, and masters should more particularly attend to this, and though in matters which respect trust, appointments to office, and the fulfilment of necessary duties, they ought to make choice of such as are best fitted to perform them, men in whom they have observed most talent, and who have proved themselves especially deserving of trust, and should, in manifesting external honour and respect, attend to the claims of each one's position, office, and disposition, according to the rule of prudence and justice; yet, in keeping up friendly and charitable intercourse with them, an equality of attention should, as far as possible, be paid to each one, so that the frequency of our communications with some may not imply contempt of others, but all may believe, and with truth, that they are loved, esteemed, and favoured as fully as real charity requires.

This is a point for parents to observe towards their children, a master with his servants, a superior with his subjects; and, in a less degree, a friend with his friends, a brother with his brothers, a subject with his equals. This care is necessary in order to remove envy, jealousies, or feelings of bitterness and ill-will between man and man, and in order to preserve the peace and union of charity amongst all. And this likewise Christ has taught us by His example. For, although in certain things He placed some Apostles before others, and did on certain occasions give marks of His love and favour to one Apostle which He did not give to another, seeing that good order and the government of the Church necessitated such differences of office and privilege, for sufficient reasons and holy ends, yet with these exceptions Christ ordinarily treated all alike, and maintained so strict an equality between them all, in His conversation and sweet address, in providing for their wants, in eating meat with them, in bearing with and listening to them, in replying and consoling, and in showing to them the bowels of His love, that during the whole time our Lord dwelt with them in His mortal life, it could not be discovered which of them was to be the head.

As to this Jansenius has well observed, when discussing the question proposed to our Lord, "*Who, thinkest Thou, is the greater in the kingdom of Heaven?*"*—"It is worthy of special notice, with how great equality our Lord treated all His disciples, for they could not at all make up their minds whom He intended to place above the rest and make their chief." St. Basil treats of the same equal balance of manner, so necessary for the preservation of peace and union: "In religious community life, all private meetings or associations are to be carefully avoided, as well as particular friendships, for from these jealousies, suspicions, and quarrels spring up."† And though greater attention may be paid to some who stand higher, and are more useful or deserving, than to others not so placed, still it behoves us to be equally moved to pity by the misfortunes of each one, and to succour him in his necessities with the like charity. Nor, should they be even relations, are we to give them anything special on that account, for in such cases of distress it is not natural affection that should sway us, but whatever conduces most to the union and edification of all.

* St. Matt. xviii. 1.
† St. Basil, *De Instit. Monach.* Serm. ii.

CHAPTER XLIV.

To what extent, and for what reason, enemies should be loved, and how excellent this duty is.

IT is found so difficult a matter to love our enemies that St. Athanasius pronounces it to be wholly above our natural strength, and Jesus Christ has instructed us in the means best suited for attaining this perfection of charity. He requires us to love our enemies, and those who hate and injure us, and to desire for them the benefits of grace and eternal glory, and all the temporal goods conducive to their salvation, and even ourselves to render all the service in our power, according to their needs. Thus, St. Augustine: "You should love your enemy, and if you do really love him, pray for him that he may share eternal glory along with you; for you are not to love him as one who is to remain your enemy, but that through grace he may become your brother." * Now to assist our enemy towards this end we must, as far as we conveniently can, help him both spiritually and temporally. "This," says St. Augustine, "is the part of true charity, that we should do good to those who hate us." †

Our enemies are, according to their nature, neighbours made after the likeness of God, capable of His glory, preserved through the infinite power and goodness of the same Lord, and redeemed through His Blood, that along with us they may be blessed in the eternal fruition of one and the same God. And more particularly ought we to love them, because Christ our God and Saviour has so willed and enjoined, in these words: "*I say to you, love your enemies; do good to them that hate you, and pray for*

* St. Aug. *In Epist. S. Joan.* tr. viii. † *Tract. de laud. Charit.*

them that persecute and calumniate you."* God had commanded the same in His written law, but not in such express terms. His precept in the Gospel is most clear and express. Who is it that thus commands us, "*Love your enemies?*" It is the Eternal and All-powerful God, Who created out of nothing, through His infinite power, the heavens and the earth, and all that they contain. He is the Supreme and Absolute Lord, Who does that which He wills, Whom all His Angels in fullest liberty, and all creatures with their whole natural strength, obey, not the very least of them departing from His will. He is the Universal Judge of the living and the dead, in Whose power it lies to assign man to his eternal punishment or reward. It is this God, this Lord, this Judge, Who lays the commandment on us that we love our enemies.

And still, to wish good to him, who wishes ill to me, is very trying and difficult of accomplishment. But, at the same time, He Who commands it is omnipotent, and affords us every aid in carrying out easily and cheerfully whatever He requires. Besides which, He confers a very high reward on those who do what He commands, for He raises them to the most excellent dignity of the sons of God, and to the most glorious inheritance of the Kingdom of Heaven, worthy of so Divine a sonship. Yet an enemy is not deserving of being loved because he is bad in himself and malicious towards others. But He Who requires us to love him is infinitely good, and infinitely holy and benevolent, and deserves that for the sake of Himself and of His love, and because of His precept, we should love our enemy, however much he is, through his own fault, unworthy of any love or any service from us. Wherefore, that most loving Master, Who enjoins this on you, has laid you under obligation by doing for you the same act of charity which He now requires of you. For, when you yourself were full of sin, His enemy, unworthy of all good, deserving eternal punishment, He loved you and drew you

* St. Matt. v. 44.

on to His friendship after, in His love, He had given His life for you; and the moment that He saw you truly contrite He not only forgave the innumerable sins by which you had dishonoured and shown your contempt of Him, but also, in a moment, remitted the whole of that eternal punishment which you had incurred on account of them.

You are therefore under a most strict obligation, after the love shown to you by a Lord of infinite beauty, glory, and majesty, whilst you were His enemy, and a most vile and base creature, to love your neighbour simply because Christ wishes and enjoins it, and to forgive one who is equal to you in nature the evil which he has done you, and which you as a sinner deserving eternal punishment have well merited. He has not explained His will and precept to you merely in the dead letter, nor has He sent His commands to you through any servant or minister, but He Himself, by His own mouth, appearing visibly in mortal flesh, has declared and notified it to you, inviting you, at the same time, to His promised reward: "*Love your enemies, that you may be the children of your Father Who is in Heaven.*"*

The obligation of loving our enemies because God commands us to do so is strong and manifold. It is an act of very great virtue to fulfil this debt, and it is a very great act of God's power to despoil the heart of man of that self-love with which it has been infected from its very source, and to imbue man with so rare a charity as to love, purely for the sake of God, one who bears hatred against him. And it is worthy of all admiration that man, naturally so weak in virtue, should be enabled to exercise so exalted a charity as to wish and act from his heart in the most kindly way towards one who is behaving very badly to him. St. Augustine, in his *Confessions*, acknowledges that there is nothing more wonderful in the history of man, than a perfect love towards his enemies. It is indeed a great virtue, and one of great price and merit before God

---

* St. Matt. v. 45.

to love from a pure motive neighbours who are friendly to us, and strangers who are virtuous; but to love in the same way neighbours who are hostile to us, and bad men who have done us injury, is a much higher virtue, and of far higher value and merit in the eyes of God. If it be simply from an equally intense love of God that the just man is moved to love his friend and his enemy, he will, in that case, love his friend with fervour and strong impulse, and his enemy with effort and with much tepidity.

It is as though one sought to kindle at the same fire a piece of wood thrust into it and well dried, and another piece only placed near it, or else quite wet; in the first case the wood would catch fire at once, in the other it would only become warm. So if a man, with the same love of God and the same amount of advertence to Him, loves his friend whom he identifies with himself and who presents no impediments to his affection, and loves his enemy kept at some distance by want of sympathy and presenting the impediment of anger and ill-will, he loves his friend with ardour and intensity, but his enemy he loves weakly and coldly. With this agrees well the opinion of doctors who maintain that love shown towards a friend is more excellent and more meritorious than that shown to an enemy, because the object beloved, when a friend, is better and more worthy of love. And so, because the love both of our friend and of our enemy springs from an equal degree of love towards God, the essential reward of our charity, as a good work, will be equal in both cases; but a greater accidental reward, corresponding to the goodness and superior excellence of the act in itself, will follow the love of a friend than will be given to the love of an enemy. For, as St. Thomas writes, the more excellent and noble the act is in which a just man has been engaged, so much the greater is its merit. The essential reward promised by God is drawn from the beatific vision, the accidental reward is the joy which the blessed will receive from their own good works.

Though what we have stated is the case when the love borne to a friend and that borne to an enemy spring from an equal degree of love to God, yet when an enemy is loved with the same strength and fervour of fraternal charity that a friend is, beyond all doubt, the love of our enemy is higher, more excellent, and of greater value and merit than the love of our friend, since it proceeds from a more perfect charity and from a stronger love of God. And just as the fire must be far more intense which kindles wood placed at a little distance, or when damp and even wet, as rapidly as if it was dry and actually laid upon it; so the degree of love to God that moves a just man to love his bitter enemy, with whom he has no sympathy, nay by whom he is repulsed, and to do this with all the fervour and completeness that he would show to a friend most united and worthy of his love, this must be a degree far stronger, better, and purer. So great excellence of love must needs rank higher and be more meritorious with God. To this fact all the saints, and Scripture itself, bear witness. Thus St. Augustine: "It is less great a work to wish well, or to act well to him who has done you no ill; but it is a grander work, and one of most perfect charity to love also your enemy, and to wish and do all the good in your power to him who has wished and done to you all the the evil in his power."* And St. Gregory says that God set so high a value on the prayers of Moses and Samuel as to put into the mouth of Jeremias these very strong words: "*If Moses and Samuel shall stand before Me, My soul is not towards this people.*"† Thus God indicated how excellent and how deserving of highest merit is that true and most deeply felt love of our enemies which these prophets exercised with so great perfection.

* St. Aug. *in Enchir.* tom. iii. cap. lxxiii.
† Jerem. xv. 1.

CHAPTER XLV.

Another reason which makes the love of our enemies so excellent, and so much more perfect than that of our friends.

THE love of a friend and of one connected with us is rich in aids and motives that make it easy and pleasant to us; such are the enjoyments of his company, the feeling of love returned, of advantage gained already, or to be gained, insomuch that the love for a friend or relative is not simply an act of charity. Whereas the love of an enemy has none of these human helps and motives, and is, on the contrary, burdened with impediments and difficulties; hence, when practised by really good men, it is generally a very pure act of charity. On this account it proves a most sincere love towards God, for while all true love of our neighbour testifies love towards God, this love of our enemy bears the fullest and strongest testimony to it, since it has no admixture of human motives in its exercise.

We should therefore esteem it as a very marked act of goodness and mercy on the part of God that His Divine Majesty affords us occasions of practising love to our enemy, and so of feeling assured that we have true love for God, since without any human considerations, and for His sake alone, we are able to love and render services to an enemy who hates and tries to injure us. This Christ meant when He said, "*If you love them only who love you, what reward shall you have? Do not even the publicans this? And if you salute your brethren only, what do you more? Do not also the heathens this?*" If you love and salute only your friends it is clear that you have not Divine charity, nor love them out of true love for God, but with merely a natural and human affection, such as is the love of sinners and of the heathen, and that in consequence no reward is due to you from God. "*Be you therefore perfect, as also your Heavenly Father is perfect.*"* Love from your heart not only your friends and those nearly connected with you, but your enemies also, for thus shall you have true charity, in which are contained both that perfection of the precept which is necessary for salvation, and that perfection which is of counsel; these will make you perfect after the similitude and likeness of your Heavenly Father.

Is it not beyond all things wonderful that God, Who is of infinite perfection, should desire, and should condescend to make creatures, imbued only with reason, like to Himself in perfection? Assuredly it is the supreme dignity of man to share in the perfection of God, and to be made like to Him. Now this complete good, this full glory, man acquires by loving his enemies from his heart, and doing good to them. And, that we may learn how to practise this love of our enemies, let us consider in order those examples which Christ our Lord has furnished to us.

CHAPTER XLVI.

In what way we ought to practise charity towards our enemies, by removing occasions of anger, and conceding our own rights in order to please them.

ONE mode of exercising charity towards an enemy is to remove every occasion likely to feed his anger when he becomes excited against us, and so prevent the guilt and scandal to souls from spreading. Our Lord gives us several instances of this. While He was still an infant, knowing that Herod was determined to take His life, and was busily laying plans to carry out his wicked designs, our Lord, instead of open resistance by causing his sudden

* St. Matt. v. 46, 48.

death, and destroying his soul in Hell, withdrew Himself
from his rage by the flight into Egypt, and thus saved him
from the terrible crime of laying his hands on the Saviour
of the world. So that, although Herod began with the
cruel slaughter of the Innocents, yet on hearing nothing
further of the Divine Child he abandoned his savage
project.

Later on, in the first year of His public ministry Christ
dwelt in Judæa, and began to baptize through the hands
of His disciples. The Pharisees on perceiving this, even
in the lifetime of St. John the Baptist, and noticing that
many more came to be baptized by Christ's disciples than
now went to St. John, became very indignant, more particularly as our Lord did this without their authority, and,
as they considered, to the injury of their credit and profits.
However holy and however useful to souls His baptism
was, our Lord restrained His disciples for a time in consequence of the opposition raised, and quitting Judæa,
though it was the head province of the country, "*He went
again into Galilee,*"* thus appeasing the wrath of the
Pharisees, and removing the occasion of it from before
their eyes.

At another time, when our Lord was about to go up
from Galilee to Jerusalem for the great feast of Tabernacles,
which lasted seven days, being aware of the strong feeling
excited against Him by the chiefs of the people, and their
intention to slay Him if possible, He remained hidden and
unknown for the first few days, until their malice was
somewhat abated, and then manifested Himself in the
Temple, publicly preaching and leading souls to Heaven.
But again, when He announced that He was the Messias
desired and expected by the Patriarchs, believed in and
hoped for by Abraham, and when the Pharisees once more in
their fury took up stones to cast at Him, that most gentle
Saviour, anxious to do them no harm, nor to remain there
lest they might go to greater lengths, passed out from the

* St. John iv. 3.

Temple unobserved through their midst, and concealed Himself from them.* Whence St. Gregory says on this passage, "What did Christ here by His own act tell us, but that, although it may be in our power to resist, still we should meekly turn aside the anger of our enemies when proudly swelling against us.†

On the occasion of His solemn entrance into Jerusalem attended by the procession of palms, whilst rebuking in the Temple the sins and the darkness of ignorance in which the rulers of the party were involved, by neither acknowledging nor making use of the light which God had given to them, the Scribes and Pharisees rose up in bitter anger against Him; and again our Lord, in order to appease them, "*went away and hid Himself from them*,"‡ and retired the same night to Bethany. St. Chrysostom assigned as the true cause of this, that our Lord knew what was in their hearts, and the unrelenting hatred which they had conceived against Him, and that, being unwilling it should as yet fully burst out upon Him, He concealed Himself till it had somewhat abated.§

What our Lord taught by these examples is that when our enemies pursue us with their violent hatred, we should, instead of meeting force with force, or going to any extremity against them, rather bear with them, and avoid such occasions as will bring out the anger and jealousy which they feel; unless, indeed, justice binds us to harsher measures, as it does those rulers and judges whose duty it is to protect the public good and punish offenders. For this purpose, should it be necessary to omit for a time even the duties of teaching or preaching, to hide some particular talent, or leave some particular place, this should be done, although that which we do out of charity may be interpreted as an act of weakness or of fear. It is far better to incur this accusation than to confirm them in their hatred or allow them to proceed to greater offence against God,

---

* St. John vii. 1. † St. Greg. Hom. xviii. *In Evang.* ‡ St. John xii. 36.
§ St. Chrysostom, Hom. lxvii. *in Joan.*

and so lose their souls; and, if appeased, they may be changed from enemies into friends. St. Paul exhorts us to what our Lord taught: "*If it be possible, as much as in you, have peace with all men; not revenging yourselves, my dearly beloved*" against injuries received, "*but give place unto the wrath*" of a neighbour "by not resisting him, and by not allowing him any pretext for his wrath."*

Let us see in what way the saints followed our Lord's example. St. Basil was attacked by the calumnies and false witness of his chief enemies, and especially of Eustathius, Bishop of Armenia, and his companions. And, although it was in his power to have at once defended himself, and by the disclosure of the malice of his opponents to have hurled back upon them their infamous accusations; yet rather than do this he held his peace, leaving himself without defence or reply, that he might exercise humility, patience, and the love of his enemies, and at the same time might soften their hostility. Thus he acted not for a few days merely, but during three whole years, until at length their obstinacy and the vindication of truth compelled him to speak; and he who had been silent in his own cause and for the good of his enemies, could not but speak out in his zeal for the glory of God. As he wrote to his own monks: "This is now the third year that I have had to endure these calumnies, but since our silence appears to tend to their greater ruin, I have for this reason undertaken to write," &c.†

How did St. Gregory of Nazianzus act in a similar case? Whilst he was Archbishop of Constantinople many persecutions were raised against him, especially that caused by certain bishops assembled in synod, who sought, out of envy, to deprive him of his dignity, and substitute another in his place. The holy man could easily have stood on his defence, and have overcome and confounded all their machinations, having on his side the cause of truth, the Emperor, the people, and many fellow-bishops of higher

* Rom. xii. 18. † Baron. *Annal.* t. iv. an. 371.

M

credit; but declining to do so, he preferred to appease his enemies, and prevent the continuance of ill-feeling between the two opposite sides. He therefore resigned the Archbishopric, which he had administered with great patience and energy, and abundant fruit, exclaiming, "If I am the cause of this serious tempest, cast me into the sea, as being no better than Jonas was;" then, quitting Constantinople, he betook himself to Nazianzus in Cappadocia, where he spent the remainder of his life in solitude, engaged in prayer, contemplation, and writing.

After this manner did the saints, in imitation of Christ, submit calmly to ignominies and injuries heaped on them, and resign their rightful claims, that they might disarm the hatred and malice of their enemies, and win them back by their humility and charity.

CHAPTER XLVII.

Our enemies are sometimes to be propitiated by explaining to them the motive of our actions.

THERE remains yet another way of appeasing our enemies, which is, to show them why we do that which offends them, and thus, convincing them by truth and right reason, put an end to their opposition. Let us look at our Lord's own example in this respect.

On a particular occasion He entered the Synagogue, that He might teach according to His wont; and it was the Sabbath-day. His enemies, laying a snare for Him, placed before Him a man "*who had a withered hand,*" in order that, after He had cured him on the Sabbath, they might accuse our Lord of transgressing the law. Christ resolved to correct their false opinion, that the cure of a man by a mere word could violate the Sabbath, and thus induce them to lay aside their false and malicious accusations. He employed this argument with them, "*What* man shall there be among you, that hath one sheep: and if the same fall into a pit on the Sabbath-day, will he not take hold on it and lift it up? How much better is a man than a sheep?"* How much more shall it be lawful to do that for a man which is done for a sheep, in delivering and saving him from the evil into which he has fallen? When, on some other Sabbath-day our Lord entered, by invitation, the house of a certain chief Pharisee to eat bread, a man afflicted with dropsy was brought to Him, to see whether He would heal him, and so give them an opportunity of accusing Him of breaking the Sabbath-day. Again, to teach them and make them ashamed of their malicious design, Christ argued with them as before, "*Which of you shall have an ass or an ox fall into a pit, and will not immediately draw him out on the Sabbath-day?*"† As though He had said, If you are willing to do this for a mere beast of burden, and deem the act lawful, lest you yourselves should suffer loss, how much more lawful is it for Me to deliver men, whom I love and value so much, out of those evils in which both their bodies and souls are lying, even though it be the Sabbath; and all the more so when, without any corporal labour, I heal them by a simple word? By such clear proof and argument as this, Christ silenced the objections of the Scribes and Pharisees, and sought to clear up their darkness of mind and cure them of their malice against Him.

By the same means He teaches us to lay before our enemies and opponents the justness, reason, and truth of our words and actions, that we may soften their feelings against us and turn them aside from the injury which they are doing to themselves as well as to us. Thus did Job treat his servants and dependents, whose complaints he listened to and carefully answered, telling them the reasons of all that he decided on. "*If I have despised to abide judgment with my manservant, or my maidservant, when*

* St. Matt. xii. 11.   † St. Luke xiv. 5.

they had any controversy against me?"* We are especially bound to follow this course with those who oppose us, not out of malice, but either from ignorance or from passionate excitement. To such we should explain our motives calmly and in modest and humble words, careful not to exaggerate their fault, however great really, but keeping strictly to truth, and making allowances for them as far as possible. In this let us copy St. Peter, who, though convicting the Jews of their horrible enormity in crucifying the Saviour of the World, yet gently excused them somewhat. "*And now, brethren, I know that you did it through ignorance, as did also your rulers.*"† For though there was this malice in their act, that they were not ignorant of our Lord's justice and innocence, yet they knew not that He was most certainly God; and so the desire not to exaggerate found this excuse for them. By a like kindness and moderation in our tone ought we to give a reason according to truth and justice to our enemies, and so turn away their anger, the Holy Ghost Himself bearing witness that "*a mild answer breaketh wrath.*"‡

CHAPTER XLVIII.

Love towards our enemies is to be preserved even while they are doing us an injury; all anger and retaliation being at once checked within us.

THE practice of charity and the forgiveness of an enemy are, ordinarily speaking, most in danger when we have just received at his hands some grievous injury in word or deed, for then the angry passion dwells within us and darkens every thought, and the devil fans our hot temper into flame, and the man whose will is weak both speaks and acts impulsively, and easily conceives a settled anger and a desire of revenge in his heart. A man must therefore be

* Job xxxi. 13.   † Acts iii. 17.   ‡ Prov. xv. 1.

well on his guard and armed against the emergency; he must be confirmed and resolute in the exercise of charity, that when the danger comes, he may stand firm in his love of his enemy and admit no hatred, no vindictive thought into his breast. We find many examples of this charity in the life of our Lord.

As the time drew near in which Christ would pass to His Father through the gate of death, He set forth from Galilee towards Jerusalem, sending certain disciples before Him as messengers to the Samaritans, whose city He intended to visit on His way and stay in it to preach His doctrine. But these Samaritans, having a contention with the Jews whether their temple on Mount Gerizim or the Temple of Jerusalem was the place appointed for the true worship of God, and observing that as the Paschal feast drew nigh "*Jesus steadfastly set His face to go to Jerusalem*," would not receive Him nor admit Him into their town, nor hear His doctrine, but rejected Him with ignominy. Yet Jesus, on seeing Himself thus repulsed and despised, allowed no feeling of indignation to rise within Him, nor was He angry with them, nor made any complaint.

But His two disciples, James and John, at sight of the grievous insult offered by these Samaritans to their Master, were moved, as they thought, with a just and holy zeal to call down merited punishment from Heaven, like the Prophet Elias of old against those who came to seize him; and "*they said, Lord, wilt Thou that we,*" in Thy Name, "*command fire to come down from Heaven and consume them?*" But He knew this zeal to be indiscreet and tainted with the spirit of vindictiveness, which they were then too unskilled in spiritual things to detect; and He saw, moreover, that, however pure such zeal might be, and well befitting the spirit of the written law (since men, for the hardness of their hearts, stood much in need of such examples of justice), yet it did not become the dispensation and law of grace that called for examples rather of gentleness and mercy, wherefore He turned to His disciples and rebuked them, saying : "*You know not of what spirit you are.*"* You know not what spirit you should be of, to what spirit you are called, and by what spirit you should be ruled, for in truth you are not called unto a subjection to the spirit of fear and servitude that would drive souls to worship God by punishment and terror, according to the spirit of the old law : you are called unto obedience to the spirit of meekness, charity, and mercy, which draws souls to God chiefly by kindness, forgiveness, and works of love. "*The Son of Man came not,*" in this His first advent, "*to destroy*" and condemn "*souls, but to save;*" not to take vengeance on sinners, and deliver them over to death and eternal perdition, but to show mercy towards them, to deliver them from the death of sin and from eternal damnation, to extend pardon to them, and fill them with the life of grace and glory. Such is the office which I came into this world to fulfil, and in fulfilling which you must imitate Me, by guiding along the way of salvation every sinner that you can, by showing pity towards all, and attracting every one to Me in the spirit of love and gentleness. It becomes you not, therefore, to call down fire from Heaven upon these Samaritans, because, seeing how distant they still are from the true worship of God, to slay them were to precipitate them all into destruction and damnation. Your part is to bear with them, to wait patiently, and then call them by the preaching of the Gospel, bringing down upon them from Heaven the fire of the Holy Spirit, by which means many of them shall be converted and saved.

By these His words and actions Christ instructs us how we are to meet injury and insult from our enemies, but of this He has given us a still more striking example. He was exposed, when on the Cross, to the greatest shame and torment from His enemies that ever man was subjected to. He was fastened by large nails to its beams, He was lifted up on it, and tortured in every limb ; His nerves were torn

* St. Luke ix. 55.

asunder, His joints dislocated, and each part of His Body was racked with pain, while calumnies and blasphemies penetrated into His Heart. And now, when the time had come that seemed to demand, for the vindication of God's honour, the infliction of the most awful judgments upon the whole race of man, a consuming fire from Heaven, or the raging flames of Hell, behold, instead, the most benign and merciful Lord manifests neither indignation nor wrath against His enemies, nor utters a single complaint of their cruel treatment! With profound grief He laments over the ruin they are bringing on themselves, and as though little heeding the injuries they heap on Him, and appearing not to feel His agonizing torments, He excuses and seeks to shield them, pleading for them with His Eternal Father in those tender words: "*Father, forgive them, for they know not what they do.*" For though indeed they know that they are sinning, yet they do not know the fearful injury they commit against God, nor the terrible punishments they are calling down upon their own souls. Although they see that He Whom they crucify is a Man of great sanctity, yet they do not recognize in Him the true, consubstantial Son of God, and the true God Himself.

O sweet words of mercy, unheard before on earth! O gentle tones of charity, richer and softer than ever have been, or ever can be breathed to men in this world! that the Lord and Master of all created things, Who could in an instant have reduced to ashes the vast machinery of the universe, all the while that He was so foully and contemptuously handled by the vilest sinners a thousand times worthy of eternal flames, not only forbore to strike or do them harm, but actually defended them and besought their pardon from His Eternal Father. Nor did He wait till their violence had passed by, and the cruelty with which they were treating Him had ceased; He delayed not till they humbled themselves, and came in penitence to sue for pardon. But at once, whilst they were heaping injury upon injury, and were the more hardened in the perversity of their mind, He took them under His protection and begged that they might be forgiven. And the mercy that He asked of His Father was not the bare remission of their sins, but that He would dispose them to receive this, granting them such efficacious help as should enable them to repent of this and of all their offences, and so obtain pardon, grace, and a return to the friendship of His Heavenly Father, and an entrance into His everlasting glory. "Who is this," says St. Anselm, "that in all His afflictions did not once open His mouth to utter complaint, or accusation, or threat, or condemnation against His enemies and tormentors, and Who, at the very last, with His own mouth, pronounced over them words of benediction such as the world had never heard before,"* praying for them, petitioning for them freedom from sin and Hell, and the highest and most precious gifts of grace and glory?

CHAPTER XLIX.

How greatly it is to the interest of the Christian that he should never retaliate an injury received.

THERE rests upon us as Christians the very gravest responsibility of practising this Divine precept, and a positive necessity that we should imitate the example of Christ. For if an injury or dishonour done to ourselves by a neighbour causes hatred or a desire of retaliation to arise in our heart, even though it should not abide there longer than it would take us to say a Hail Mary, yet, inasmuch as it is voluntarily consented to, and a distinct desire of serious evil to him has been formed, a mortal sin has been committed. As an arrow when it pierces the heart, though it does so in flight and but for an instant, yet causes death, so a desire consented to, however momentarily, constitutes a mortal sin that kills the soul, alienates it from God and

* St. Anselm, *In Spec.* cap. xii.

deprives it of grace, and exposes it to eternal damnation. For the words of St. John are clear: "*He that loveth not*" his neighbour "*abideth in the death*" of his soul. "*Whosoever hateth his brother, is a murderer.*"* He is a murderer of his neighbour, as far as his will and desire goes, and of himself in very deed and act, for he actually kills his own soul.

How serious is the harm which that man does to himself who seeks to be avenged for an injury received. Hear the written law of God: "*Seek not revenge, nor be mindful of the injury of thy citizens.*"† "*Remember not any injury done thee by thy neighbour; and do thou nothing by deeds of injury.*"‡ "*He that seeketh to revenge himself shall find vengeance from the Lord, and He will surely keep his sins in remembrance.*"§ Now what will He, Who thus warns under the written law, do under the law of grace, considering that He has taught and invited us by His example and patient submission to the most cruel inflictions, to bear injuries without a thought of vengeance, but, on the contrary, both feel in our heart and manifest in our actions true charity towards him? After St. Peter had distinctly affirmed, "*Christ suffered for us, leaving you an example that you should follow His steps,*" he very soon after added the point of imitation—"*Not rendering evil for evil, nor railing for railing, but contrariwise blessing,*" and doing good; "*for unto this are you called*" by the Christian faith "*that you may inherit a blessing.*"|| In this also are you planted, that bearing evil and doing good, and returning blessing for cursing, you may through these acts of charity inherit the highest and richest blessing in the Kingdom of Heaven. We cannot doubt that the desire to retaliate on one who has wronged us, besides being a very grievous sin in itself, becomes a much more grievous offence, and will be much more heavily punished by God, in consequence of the very great benefits bestowed on us

---

* 1 St. John iii. 14, 15.   † Levit. xix. 18.   ‡ Ecclus. x. 6.
§ Ecclus. xxviii. 1. || 1 St. Peter ii. 21; iii. 9.

in the Incarnation and Passion of Him Who thus binds us to forgive, both by His own example and the very clear expression of His will.

Theodoret relates of James, the holy Bishop of Nisibis, that when the city was besieged by the imposing force of the King of Persia, in which many elephants were employed, the citizens, being hard pressed, besought the holy man to mount the battlements and call down the curse of God on the besiegers. On his way to carry out their request, the Bishop, reflecting within himself that, though the defence of their town was lawful, a vindictive imprecation of evil on the enemy would not be so, instead of carrying out his first design, besought God to send an army of gnats amongst them, which might both save the city with the least amount of injury to their opponents, and show forth the power of the Divine protection over the Christians. Immediately multitudes of these insects infested the besiegers, attacking the elephants and the ears and nostrils of their horses, and the whole army was thrown into such confusion that it became necessary for the King to raise the siege and to retire. The slaughter of an enemy, if necessary for the defence of a city, is made lawful by that motive, but not by a spirit of mere vindictiveness, and it ceases to be lawful when a city can be otherwise protected. The act therefore of this holy Bishop warns us against satisfying a vindictive feeling, and should another's hostility throw us on our self-defence, we must still injure him as little as possible, for thus shall we secure ourselves against acting in a spirit of either hatred or desire of revenge.

And, as St. Augustine reminds us, moderation especially befits private individuals, for these have received no real obligation or authority to punish the guilty. Those with whom this authority lies may lawfully inflict to the full that just punishment which the good of the community requires. Thus much the charity which we owe to our enemies demands of us, and also the example left us by

Christ, that neither before, nor after, nor even at the time when injury is done us, we desire evil to him who inflicts it. Obedience to this principle frees us from the guilt and sin of revenge, and from those eternal punishments by which it shall be visited, and it exercises that most excellent virtue of charity, which is highly pleasing to God, and makes us worthy to inherit His eternal kingdom.

CHAPTER L.

We must fully forgive the injury done us by a neighbour, because charity requires this of us.

AT the moment of receiving an injury from another we are to restrain the vindictive feelings that may arise in our breast, but charity requires of us yet a further act of self-denial, for after the evil has been done we must forgive our enemy from our hearts. Here again we may look to Christ as our guide: "*If thy brother sin against thee, reprove him; and if he do penance, forgive him. And if he sin against thee seven times in a day, and seven times in a day be converted to thee, saying, I repent; forgive him.*"* To forgive an injury is to abstain from the wish that any harm whatever should, either from oneself or through another, befall an enemy, by way of compensation for damage done, or the gratification of wounded feeling, or the alleviation of the sense of pain and humiliation, for all these motives are tinged with vindictiveness, and admit of no real justification.

The certainty of this does not stand in the way of a just restitution and satisfaction in proportion to actual loss sustained, if our enemy be capable of this; for instance, he may have deprived us of something which he is able to return, to the exact value of what he took. Or he may have injured our reputation by bearing false witness against

* St. Luke xvii. 3, 4.

us, which he can restore again by now declaring the truth, in which case to demand that restitution which is an act of simple justice implies neither vindictiveness nor fault of any kind. But if the injury done to us admits of no such restitution, to insist then on punishment and disgrace by way of compensation and solace, is distinctly to be determined on vengeance; and whatever pretext of justice may be set up, it is a sin against the charity which we owe to our enemy. In favour of a full pardon of all offences against us, Christ urges on us this strong argument: "*With what measure you mete, it shall be measured to you again.*"* If you pardon those sins which your neighbour has committed against you, your Heavenly Father will forgive you those sins which you have committed against Him; but if you refuse forgiveness to those who have injured you, your Father will also refuse to forgive you.

That He might make this most important comparison and motive still plainer, and still more forcible, our Lord confirmed it with the following simile: "*The Kingdom of Heaven is likened to a king who would take an account of his servants, and one was brought to him that owed him ten thousand talents. And as he had not wherewithal to pay it,*" he besought the king for mercy and forbearance. "*And the lord of that servant let him go, and forgave him that debt. But when he was gone out, he found one of his fellow-servants that owed him a hundred pence,*" whom, after all his entreaties, he refused to spare, or even to allow time for repayment, but "*cast him into prison, till he should pay the debt.*" The king hearing of this, called his ungrateful servant into his presence, and said to him: "*Thou wicked servant, I forgave thee all the debt, because thou besoughtest me; shouldst not thou then have had compassion also on thy fellow-servant, even as I had compassion on thee? And his lord being angry, delivered him to the torturers until he should pay all the debt.*"† And as all that debt could not possibly be paid, because being due to God it

* St. Matt. vii. 2. † St. Matt. xviii. 23, seq.

was in a manner infinite, so must those torments also last for ever. This ungrateful servant represents the sinner, who owes to God the immense debt incurred by his sins, yet if found by Him to be penitent, is forgiven all, through His infinite mercy, but he, on receiving in his turn an injury from his fellow-men, which, however grievous in his eyes, is comparatively slight, as being an offence only against man, will not forgive it. God, in His anger against the sinner, condemns him to eternal punishment, whence our Lord concludes with these words : "*So also shall My Heavenly Father,*" in the earnestness of His justice, "*do to you, if you forgive not every one his brother from your hearts.*" For neither will He forgive you the debt left by your sins, but will, on account of it, deliver you over to the torturers in Hell, that you may burn along with them in everlasting flames.

Our minds cannot grasp the full force of this argument. For what better thing could happen to the sinner, who has offended God and incurred His anger, than that he should appease that same God, be restored to His favour and friendship, be delivered from eternal damnation, and find access again to His heavenly glory? So exceeding great would be this good, that were we, in order to obtain it, to traverse barefooted the whole earth, to walk on thorns, to practise all the mortifications of the holy confessors, or undergo all the tortures of the martyrs, all these would be as nothing. How inconceivably immense is the evil of losing God and His glory for ever, and of burning in never-ending fire! And yet by simply forgiving the injury done us by a neighbour, for the sake of God, and in the spirit of penance for all our own sins, the sinner is able to deliver himself from so immense an evil and acquire so infinite a good.

With how great promptitude and alacrity of mind, then, ought a man to pardon every injury received by him, and desire that many opportunities of so doing may be granted to him, without however any offence to the

Most High, thus placing constantly in his hands fresh sacrifices to offer to God! St. Augustine writes, "Let it not be difficult to you, brethren, but most easy, to forgive your enemies and to pray for them; because in no other way can we hope to obtain pardon for ourselves from God, except by fully pardoning every kind of injury done to us. There is no higher sacrifice which we owe to God, than to do all the good in our power even to evilly-inclined men, and to our own particular enemies above all, for the sake of God."* What need of arousing the apathetic sinner with the awful thunder of these words: "*If you will not forgive men, neither will your Father forgive you your offences!*"† Oh, with how great reason did St. Augustine again exclaim: "He who awakens not at so terrible a sound, is not asleep, but dead; even then, since God has power to raise the dead to life, let him rise and do penance, and forgive that he may be forgiven."‡

In consideration of the extreme importance for the Christian life of this exercise of charity, it has pleased God to mark by very portentous facts the punishment measured out to those who refuse to forgive. As for instance, that He Himself refuses to pardon them either in this life, or the next, but suffers them to die in their impenitence. Blessed Lysiardus, Bishop of Soissons, speaks of a noble and wealthy lady, who conceived so intense a hatred against certain enemies for the murder of her husband and only son, that she vowed and thirsted to have her revenge. When a holy man came and begged her, for the sake of her own soul, and for the consolation of those whose death she mourned, to pardon her enemies, she resisted all his entreaties. Now, even though the cause of this woman's anger was so grave as the death of her own child and husband, yet her determination not to forgive so offended God, that after the departure of this holy man a terrific storm fell upon her house, levelled

---

* St. Aug. lib. l. hom. vi.   † St.
‡ St. Aug. *In Enchir.*

it with the ground, and buried in its ruin this miserable woman in the midst of her impenitence. And to make this a still more evident judgment upon her sin, although in the same house were many male and female servants, and many birds and animals kept close beside it, every one of these escaped unhurt, their mistress alone was struck down and "buried in Hell."

Similar judgments God has sent, and still sends against hardened sinners, who cannot bring themselves to forgive an injury. He suffers them to die in their sins, and cuts short their lives in their impenitence. Let us then, in common prudence, fear these judgments of God, and let as turn to account the unspeakable mercy which He as yet extends to us, granting pardon for every injury, in order that pardon may be granted to us. "*Forgive thy neighbour if he hath hurt thee, and then shall thy sins be forgiven to thee when thou prayest.*"*

CHAPTER LI.

It does not become those who have suffered an injury, to desire its punishment on the ground of justice, even for a good end.

WE have hitherto spoken of the strict obligation which charity lays on the Christian, of pardoning an injury done him by an enemy. Let us now consider whether it is only a vindictive spirit that is condemned, and whether the man who would be faithful to grace may not, on the ground of justice, wish an enemy to be punished, in order to attain some good end. It most certainly is lawful to desire and obtain, for the sake of justice, the punishment of an enemy, in order to attain this good end, namely, that he may be corrected and may refrain from doing further injury, and that others may learn to fear, and be

* Ecclus. xxviii. 2.

deterred from following his example; for these results concern the public good, which comes before the private good of the individual. But although this is lawful, and is therefore incumbent on judges and such public officers as are bound to consult and protect the good of the community, yet it is not befitting that private persons who have received some injury should, out of justice, inflict punishment on an enemy.

And the first reason is that, ordinarily speaking, these persons have not their passions under such control as to prevent the admixture of some vindictiveness with the good end which they propose. A clear indication of this is that, when an enemy has, in the interests of justice, to be punished, they bestow far more labour and money in securing that end, than they are found to do in matters more simply and directly connected with the public good and the benefit of souls. Better proof could not be given that in seeking the punishment of an enemy, it is not purely the benefit of the community, but the gratification of private resentment that they have most at heart. It is not right, then, that men should, even on the ground of justice, aim at punishing an enemy, unless they are singularly mortified in their passions and fervent in charity; let them rather freely pass over the injury, and allow the restoration of justice to be seen to by those to whom the duty belongs. St. Augustine, writing on these words of Christ : "*But I say to you not to resist evil,*" says : "That vengeance or punishment which is decreed by those having authority is not forbidden here, for such tends to the correction of evil, and is not vindictiveness, but mercy. Its infliction, however, is to be committed only to him, who through the strength of his love has overcome the passion which generally burns in the breast of persons most desirous of taking vengeance into their own hands."*
The first reason therefore for denying this right of punishment to the injured person is that what appears to him to

---

* St. Aug. *In Serm. Dom. in Monte*, cap. xx.

be zeal for justice is too often passion, vindictiveness, and a serious fault.

A second reason is that, if the good of souls be really intended, a man will succeed far more in edifying and assisting them by the example of his charity and readiness to forgive, than he will in correcting them through the terrors of justice. Besides which, the commonwealth gains more from examples of charity in forgiving injuries, this being repugnant to our natural inclinations and so the virtue of the few, than it does from examples of punishing injuries in the cause of justice, for to this all men are naturally inclined, and often find it a snare for the secret indulgence of their own angry passions. St. Gregory Nazianzen furnishes us in his own life with a very strong confirmation of this. When his adversaries were assailing him with the bitterest persecutions, and had nearly stoned him to death while saying Mass, but for the miraculous interposition of God, Theodorus the Bishop wished to obtain their condign punishment, they being under his jurisdiction, and begged permission from the Saint to do this; but he received for answer that, although some good would be gained by yielding his consent, as their punishment might strike terror into others, yet it would be far better for himself and far more pleasing to God that they should be pardoned. And on this point he afterwards enlarged, saying: "Much, we are of opinion, may be gained by the punishment of those who have injured us, for this is very useful in correcting the faults of others. But it is much nobler, and makes us more like to God, to bear meekly the injuries inflicted on us: the former act, indeed, holds wickedness in check, but this one attracts men to virtue, a gain far greater than the mere abstention from sin. We esteem it a truly great work of brotherly kindness to forgive what has been done against us, that we ourselves may obtain mercy from God."* To the same effect writes St. Paul to the Corinthians: "*There is plainly a fault among*

---

* Baron. *Annal.* t. iv. ann. 389.

you, that you have lawsuits one with another," that is, quarrels needing to be referred to the public tribunals. You will perhaps say that some of you are free from blame in this matter. But, in order to be really blameless, "*Why do you not rather take wrong? Why do you not rather suffer yourselves to be defrauded,*"* than thus go to law to obtain satisfaction at the hands of justice? And though in many cases appeal to the law is necessary for the sake of due redress, yet mere personal injuries, such as we are now treating of, should be borne with and forgiven, in order to please and serve God.

CHAPTER LII.

We have no right to rejoice in the misfortunes of an enemy, but should feel for and commiserate him.

A STILL more perfect act of charity towards our enemies is to sympathize with them in their distresses, instead of feeling any joy or satisfaction in their having to suffer. For as the pleasure which we feel in a neighbour's good is an act of love, so to take pleasure in his misfortune is a sign of hatred. Holy Scripture most strongly denounces, and God Himself punishes with especial severity, a sin of hatred such as this. "*When thy enemy shall fall, be not glad; and in his ruin let not thy heart rejoice; lest the Lord see, and it displease Him, and He turn away His wrath from him,*"† and the evil in which thou rejoicest, and fasten it upon thee.

It is not a fault, but it is even laudable to rejoice in the death of the wicked, on account of the benefit thence arising to the good in being thus delivered out of their hands, as well as of the greater glory accruing to God in the manifestation of His providence and the fear inspired by His justice, besides the spiritual gain to our enemy himself, who may, as we hope, take warning at the last moment;

* 1 Cor. vi. 7.   † Prov. xxiv. 17, 18.

for these reasons holy men in the old dispensation were glad at the death or overthrow of the enemies of the people of God, and were moved to sing their hymns of joy.* But if, on the other hand, this joy over the destruction of an enemy is felt simply because he is our enemy, and because the evil which has befallen him is fitting payment for the injury which he has done to us, it is changed into a great sin, lying under the condemnation of the Divine law. And it is of rejoicing such as this that the Wise Man says: "*He that rejoiceth at another man's ruin, shall not be unpunished.*"† Our weapon against this vice must be the contrary act of charity and mercy, in compassionating and grieving most sincerely over the spiritual and temporal misfortunes of our enemies. Not less than this does Christ teach us from His own acts.

St. Luke tells us that while on the feast of Palms our Lord was being conducted with honour and triumph into Jerusalem, "*When He drew near, seeing the city, He wept over it.*" He seems to have paused a while that He might dwell in sad thought on the future scenes of His Passion, ever present to His mind, when the rulers of the people would let loose all their hatred and malice upon Him, and the fickle populace would take up their cry, and such dreadful crimes would be perpetrated, and when all would be closed in by the fearful temporal and eternal judgments sent forth on them by the Divine justice. He did not weep over the torments and ignominies which He Himself would so willingly undergo, but on the evils coming upon the city that lay beneath His eyes, and upon the men whose deadly hatred would not rest till they had nailed Him to the Cross. And though He had hitherto borne about with Him this grief locked within His own breast, on that day He willed that it should burst forth copiously with His tears, like one whose sobs can no longer be repressed. "*If thou also hadst known, and that in this thy day, the things that are to thy peace, but now they are hidden*

---

* Psalm cviii.   † Prov. xvii. 5.

from thine eyes."[*] He would say, if thou, O city of Jerusalem, wouldst but learn, as thou shouldst do, those things that concern thy true peace, and thy spiritual and eternal happiness, in place of those that concern the temporal peace and prosperity which thou now enjoyest! If thou wouldst but know the good things that are now offered thee, for acquiring and possessing the true peace of redemption and the forgiveness of thy sins, the adoption of the sons of God, victory over thy vices and passions, and that belief and obedience in My word which would give thee a share in My merits! Oh, couldst thou but see these good things appointed for thy real good, in this day in which I have discoursed of them in thy midst, and am come to suffer even unto death in thy streets, in this day in which thou hast still time and opportunity to make use of them; but alas! in thy sin and blindness thou wilt not acknowledge them. Wherefore, "*the days shall come upon thee, and thy enemies shall cast a trench about thee, and compass thee round, and straiten thee on every side,*" so that, none being able to pass forth, all within thee shall perish, since none from without can come to succour thee. And all this was fulfilled when their city was surrounded by the Romans, and reduced to such straits that the unhappy Jews, in unheard-of sufferings and famine, were driven to feed on every kind of animal and filth, and at length on one another, and even mothers on their own offspring.

Our Lord continues His prophecy: "*They shall beat thee flat to the ground,*" and shall destroy thy walls and thy houses, "*and they shall not leave in thee a stone upon a stone, and thy children who are in thee*" shall be consumed, some by famine, and some by the sword, and others sold for slaves; "*because thou hast not known the time of thy visitation.*" I came indeed, sent by My Heavenly Father for thy good and for that of all men. I came to build thee up again and to save thee and all the world, to deliver thee from the death of sin and eternal punishment, and from

[*] St. Luke xix. 42.

every kind of evil, and to confer the life of grace and glory upon thee; yet so obstinate have been thy malice and blindness that thou hast refused to acknowledge thy Saviour, Who hath come to visit thee in such Divine love and mercy. After this manner did Christ enter with the profoundest grief into the spiritual, temporal, and eternal evils of His enemies, and this His grief and compassion He exhibited openly to others by tears from His sacred eyes, thus teaching us by His own example, not to rejoice over the misfortunes of our enemies, but to sympathize with them, and desire their rescue out of them. And this the saints of God have ever faithfully performed.

Amongst other cases of persecution was that of St. Catharine of Siena, whom a certain woman maligned with a false accusation of immodesty. Although this most pure Virgin felt deeply so terrible an injustice, yet when her accuser was struck down with a disease that rendered her body too loathsome for any to venture to approach her, the Saint not merely forbore from rejoicing at, but felt compassion for, her wretched state, went and attended upon her with the utmost care and devotedness, softened her heart by the tender and loving care with which she attended on all her wants, and at last by the fervour of her prayers to God for her soul, obtained her pardon and salvation. In the like manner, therefore, must we imitate Christ, as this great Saint did, and as all the holy servants of God have done, by feeling sympathy even with our enemies in their sufferings, fulfilling towards them the exhortation of the Apostle : "*Rejoice with them that rejoice, weep with them that weep.*" * For if we rejoice with our neighbour in his prosperity, we add to his joy; and if we grieve along with him, we strengthen and are a help to him in bearing his sorrows.

* Romans xii. 15.

CHAPTER LIII.

We should not cause even shame or vexation to our enemies by way of slight retaliation, but be ready always to console them.

THERE are many persons who, although not seeking to be actually avenged on their enemies, and not rejoicing over their misfortunes, do, notwithstanding, think it fair to humble and vex them for the evil they have done them. If this shame and confusion is simply and sincerely desired with the view of drawing their attention to their fault and leading them to repent of it, then an act of true charity is rendered to them. But if the real motive for wishing an enemy to be put to shame is to embitter his feelings and obtain some compensation and satisfaction for what he has done to us, then we are bound to refrain from it, as an act of pure spite. And we must do this, if we are to imitate the example of our Lord.

When, for instance, the Scribes and Pharisees brought to our Lord the "*woman taken in adultery*," hoping to find a fresh opportunity of calumniating Him and denouncing Him as a violator of the law, in their expectation that He would not condemn her, "*Jesus, bowing Himself down, wrote with His finger on the ground,*" then lifting Himself up, "*He said to them, He that is without sin among you, let him first cast a stone at her.*"* By these words, and by what He wrote on the ground, He placed their sins before them. Fearing therefore lest He might disclose them, each one went out, leaving the woman alone. Had our Lord

* St. John viii. 7.

marked them with searching eye as each one left, He would have overwhelmed them with shame and confusion, wherefore that He might not subject them to this, "*Again stooping down, He wrote on the ground,*" as though not observing their departure, till all had gone and the woman stood alone. In imitation of Christ, we should treat our enemies in the same way. We might indeed put them to shame, showing the folly of their words or actions, at any stain upon their birth and character, or the insignificance of their appearance, or any other taunt which men feel keenly. But we have made up our minds to do nothing of the kind, nor as far as we can help shall we allow others to do it, nay, we will defend their honour and good name according to the law of charity, and the spirit and example of all good men.

The Count St. Elzear, as the history of his holy life narrates, experienced many indignities from his subjects. They tried to strip him of his authority, they laid false accusations against him, they wrote letters full of contumely and lies to injure his reputation, and these came into his hands. Yet, when the Prince of Taranto was about to put those wicked men to death by hanging and quartering, he would not allow it, since, as the injury was his, with him lay the power to forgive; but, on the contrary, he visited, spoke with them, received them into his own house, and behaved to them with all kindness, as though they had always loved and served him faithfully. And when his wife suggested that, without taking rigorous measures against them, he should at least show them the letters that had fallen into his hands, and make them feel thoroughly ashamed of themselves at finding they were detected, he resolutely refused to do so, urging the pain and disgrace it would cause them, and saying he would rather leave them under the impression that he was ignorant of their infamous proceedings. With this rare charity of the holy Count towards his enemies God was so well pleased, that He moved all his enemies to repentance for their crimes, giving them grace to amend their lives, and to vie with each other in doing honour to him as their lord, and in loving him as a father.

God has especially enjoined on us kindness and affability, even to our enemies, "*Grieve not thy brother.*"* "*Thou shalt not molest a stranger, nor afflict him.*" † And if it be needful to bring him to the point of grieving over and acknowledging his fault so as to correct it, even then we should not wish to sadden him for the sake of doing so, or of taking any pleasure in it, but should think only of the great good we hope it may do in leading him to repentance and others to amendment of life. This the Apostle signifies to the Corinthians: "*Although I made you sorrowful by my epistle, I do not repent.*" Nay, "*I am glad, not because you were made sorrowful, but because you were made sorrowful unto penance.*" ‡ And since sorrow like this cannot be avoided, the same Apostle earnestly prays the Thessalonians: "*For which cause comfort one another; and edify one another, as you also do,*" § both by holy conversations and good example.

CHAPTER LIV.

We should continue our good offices of charity towards a neighbour, even though we receive but small signs of friendship in return.

NOT a few persons of sincere piety are careful to avoid wishing any evil to an enemy, but are very easily offended if a neighbour is either not so bland or courteous to them as he is to another, or has perhaps refused some kind service asked of him, or has shown a little hostility on some particular point. They are inclined in consequence to withhold the usual marks of friendship from such, on

* Levit. xxv. 14. † Exodus xxii. 21.
‡ 2 Cor. vii. 8. § 1 Thess. v. 11.

the plea of treating them as they themselves are treated by them. Thus we hear the remark: Such a person was stiff and distant to me, I shall be the same with him; he denied me such and such a favour, so he cannot expect me to go out of my way to do him a kindness; or he never calls upon me now, and therefore it is not to be expected that I should visit him.

There is a certain vindictiveness in these little acts of uncharitableness, and they are also a clear indication that courtesies previously shown had for their motive, not God, but some personal gratification or profit. One who wishes to serve God sincerely should not suffer himself to be overcome by this temptation, but should do his best to keep up an old friendship, continuing his visits and expressions of good will and observing ordinary civilities. However much the other may have changed, let him now do purely for God, what before he had done partly for man's sake, and instead of looking for any temporal advantage let him seek a return from God and the spiritual benefit of his soul. It is the especial work of the Holy Spirit, by doing good to convert an enemy into a friend, and by works of charity to restore instead of weakening a friendship that has grown cold, provided it be one that is not hurtful to the soul.

This office of charity Christ also teaches by His own example, for while passing through the towns and villages of Judæa, preaching and working miracles, many persons followed Him with their calumnies and falsehoods, being unwilling to receive His doctrine. At length their malice proceeded so far that they planned to cast Him down the mountain-side, and ascribed the greatest amongst His miracles, which God alone could work, to the agency of the prince of the devils. Well might God have abandoned them in their wickedness and ingratitude, and have turned to the Gentiles or Samaritans, who He knew would receive Him with greater faith and reverence, and would desire greater profit from His teaching and miracles. Yet our Lord instead of doing this, on the contrary increased the benefits and mercies which He heaped upon His own people.* After He had traversed the towns and villages of Israel, calling the Twelve Apostles and seventy-two disciples He furnished them with wisdom and grace to preach His Gospel, and with power to cure all manner of diseases, to cast out devils, to restore sight to the blind and life to the dead. He then sent them throughout the whole country, to instruct and enlighten minds and heal the sick; bidding them not to go "*into the way of the Gentiles, and into the cities of the Samaritans enter ye not. But go ye rather to the lost sheep of the house of Israel*," lost in their rebellion and ingratitude.† And upon the footsteps of His disciples our Lord Himself followed, scattering abroad the same blessings and mercies as heretofore.

Although the sons of Israel showed themselves just as inhospitable to Christ and as malevolent as they had previously done, yet He was not angry with them, He did not despise them, He neither cut short nor interrupted the constant flow of His graces, but persevered in and added to their number. Thus St. Chrysostom remarks: " By sending His disciples to them Christ seems distinctly to say: Do not imagine that I feel any anger against these Jews, or that My Heart is turned away from them, because they assail Me with this contumely and say that I am possessed with a devil. So far from this, you see Me taking such care of them that I send you forth, not to others, but first of all to them, to be both their instructors and physicians; nor do I only bid you preach to them rather than to others, but I prohibit you from entering even on the way that leads to others."‡ In this, writes Euthymius, Christ exhibits the strength of His love and the greatness of His care over us, for though He was persecuted with so much cruelty, yet forgetful of all this He employed the utmost diligence in correcting and in healing them, treating them with the same kindness

---

* St. Luke iv. v. vi.   † St. Matt. x. 5, 6.
‡ St. Chrysost. Hom. xxxiii. *In Matt.* ix.

and loading them with the same favours that He would have done had they in place of injuries made Him a return of the most grateful service.

Our Lord has given us another example of the same spirit of charity. Going up to Jerusalem at the time of the feast of Tabernacles, He entered the Temple and spent the whole day in teaching the people, illuminating and consoling them by the light and grace of His doctrine. Here again, instead of gratitude, the only return they made was to plot His death and declare that He had a devil: "*The rulers and Pharisees sent ministers to apprehend Him.*" This gave rise to our Lord's question: "*Why seek you to kill Me?*" When the people answered: "*Thou hast a devil; who seeketh to kill Thee?*" To this the Evangelist subjoins: "*They sought therefore to apprehend Him, and no man laid hands on Him, because His hour was not yet come.*"* They wished indeed to seize our Lord, but were unable to do so, because He did not yet give them permission. And after He had been the whole day in the Temple, and found none in Jerusalem to give Him shelter, when evening was come "*Jesus went unto Mount Olivet,*" at the distance of two miles from the city, and there passed the night in prayer. "*And early in the morning He came again into the Temple,*" † that He might instruct, and build up, and strengthen those who came to hear Him; and although He had been treated with such insult the day before and threatened with actual violence, yet no sign is there about Him of either anger or offence taken, He is wholly occupied with His usual works of charity and beneficence.

Again, on the day of Palms our Lord is conducted with solemn procession into Jerusalem and enters the Temple. Another day He spends there, preaching and working miracles, for many blind, lame, and afflicted with various sicknesses are brought to Him, and He healed them all. Still is He followed with calumnies, still is

* St. John vii. 30.   † St. John viii. 1, 2.

He threatened with death, and at the return of night there are none to invite Him to their homes, so that He goes forth to seek shelter at Bethania. This does not prevent His return next morning, once more to teach and in the most perfect charity labour for the salvation of their souls. Three more days are devoted to sowing the seeds of His unspeakable mercies in word and in work, receiving in return only fresh attacks with the treacherous intent of catching Him in His words and finding pretext for His death. But our Lord's patience and endurance could never be worn out, nor the channel of His mercies dried up, for their lying accusations were to Him as Divine praises, and their treachery as though this had been the most devoted service it was in their power to render. Thus our Lord persevered during those three days, till on the fifth day He came to celebrate the Paschal Supper and to be put to death for these very men and for all mankind.

By such examples as these Christ has instructed us that, though we perhaps meet with only coldness or even positive insult from men whom we have laid under an obligation to us by acts of kindness, yet our duty is to remit in no respect our former goodwill or friendliness of manner towards them. The Wise Man exhorts us to the same: "*Thy own friend,*" to whom thou hast begun to show kindness, "*and thy father's friend,*" who has continued to you his old friendship, "*forsake not;*"* break off the friendship of neither, but by fresh attentions preserve it. And this advice of the Wise Man applies especially when our friendship is imperilled by the first signs of ill-feeling, for then our charity is all the greater if, refraining from any coldness ourselves, we resolutely continue all our marks of friendship. In this we shall always have for our guides those holy men who have walked in our Lord's own footsteps.

The history of the Franciscan Order tells us of a

* Prov. xxvii. 10.

holy man, Frate Masseo, one of the first disciples of St. Francis, whose charity towards his enemies was so great, that whatever injuries they might heap on him, he always loved them, and never lost an opportunity of rendering them some good office or kind act. Yet, on perceiving his love to be not quite so ready and so perfect towards some who had done him an injury, and that he took not so much pleasure in them as in his friends, he grieved much over this weakness of charity, and besought God very earnestly and perseveringly till he obtained from Him the grace of loving this enemy from whom he had received the injury with as hearty and complete a goodwill, and with as much pleasure in speaking well of him, as he did those friends who had always shown him kindness. To this charity the saints attain by the help and grace of Christ our Lord. For since in each thing they desire the fulfilment of God's will and His greater glory, they draw down the grace which disposes them to the exercise of charity where the need is greater, and victory over themselves is more signal, whence, also, the pleasure and glory of God are greatly enhanced; and this is certainly the case when an enemy is beloved with as much will and fervour as a friend can be.

CHAPTER LV.

That we may avoid scandal, a former friend is still to be spoken to and saluted, as though he had not become our enemy.

THE rule which we have given for the imitation of Christ in continuing all the offices of charity to one whose friendship we have unfortunately lost, is of especial application to our manner towards him in public, saluting and speaking to him should we happen to meet him. To refuse this were to cause remark and give scandal to any observer who, knowing of our former friendship, would detect at once the enmity that had arisen. Such a discovery disedifies and does harm, and should therefore be prevented. In this matter the Apostle warns us, "*Give no offence to any man*,"* as though he had said, avoid every fault by which you may give bad example to your neighbour, or may be the occasion to him of any sin. As again, "*From all appearance of evil refrain yourselves*,"† not merely from that which is positively sinful before God, but even that which wears the appearance or semblance of evil, or gives rise to a just suspicion, and so places a scandal in another's way. The Apostle would not have us give way to the difficulty we may feel in speaking to one with whom we are no longer friends, lest those seeing it take scandal, and conclude there must be some great cause for what seems an actual feud between us. For, as the same Apostle writes to the Romans, we ought to "*Provide good things, not only in the sight of God, but also in the sight of all men*."‡ By which he means that we are not only in our good works to satisfy conscience in those points which God sees, to Whose eyes all things are manifest, but we are to satisfy our own conscience and the will of God in those things that are open to the eyes of men. This necessitates our preserving the good that we do so free from all admixture or appearance of evil that no one can ever from an insufficient reason either condemn or suspect us. In all which our motive should be God's glory and our neighbour's profit.

This law of charity in a particular degree binds us to conquer the repugnance which we naturally feel in extending our marks of friendship to former friends who have been either assisted by us, or have received some great favour at our hands. To take another point, it is easy to convince good Christians how becoming it is in theory that those who shook hands and spoke to each other before they ceased to be friends, should say something to each other afterwards. But the precise difficulty

---

* 2 Cor. vi. 3.   † 1 Thess. v. 22.   ‡ Romans xii. 17.

is this: which of the two is to make the first advance, each wishing that the other should begin, on the ready plea that he himself is the more worthy of the two, or has been more injured, or some such excuse as self-love may dictate. In which state of doubt the first thing to observe is that, which ever side by refusing to salute the other gives scandal to the bystanders, is bound for that one reason alone to speak to him, and though the other side, being equally bound, is equally faulty in not doing his duty, this does not make his sin less a sin. So that whilst both are under obligation not to offend God, both should be equally prompt to anticipate, and not wait for the other. And he is the real gainer who is the first to fulfil his duty.

The next thing to observe is, that one ought not to consult his own convenience, nor yet human respect, but the service of God and the good of souls. And as when a king demands some service from his attendants in which he is known to take great pleasure, each one should strive to be first in rendering it, not waiting for any other; or when at the same instant the opportunity is offered to several merchants of making some very profitable investment, each one struggles to be first with his money, little caring for the rest; in like manner the charitable act whereby an adversary receives a kindly greeting is so well-pleasing to God, and is so earnestly required of us by God, as well as being of the highest profit and merit to the soul, that each one should strive and do his utmost to be first in performing it. St. Chrysostom puts this well before us: "When we reflect how great are the benefits which we draw from it, and how much it increases our confidence in God, and, above all, that the forgiveness of those who have injured us is to a certain degree an obliteration of our past sins, surely we shall spend our every energy to do them all the service that we possibly can."* Say not, It is he who has injured me, and therefore it belongs to him to be the first to speak.

* St. Chrysost. *In Gen.* cap. ix. hom. xxvii.

For if this friendship is to be regained, out of regard for God and for His glory, it is far more useful and profitable for you, the offended person, to take the first step, and invite the other to reconciliation. This will gain you a double crown of glory, one as having borne an injury with patience, the second as having won back the friendship of him who had injured you. Hasten to be beforehand with your adversary, and be the first to speak, lest he snatch the crown out of your hand by first accosting, and inviting you to be reconciled. Be drawn to this by the example of Christ our Lord and Saviour, Who, whilst we were enemies, and subjected Him to terrible injuries and insults, sought us out, spoke to us, was the first to bless us, to call and press us to accept His friendship. "*I stand at the door of your hearts and knock*," and ask for entrance—such are His gracious words. And when He was clothed with our mortal flesh, He went about on the earth, seeking lost man, who by separation from God and by sin had become His enemy, and by His words, His actions, and His loving caresses, asked for our love and drew us to His grace.

All this He testifies by the mouth of Isaias, saying: "*They have sought Me that before asked not for Me; they have found Me that sought Me not*," because I first sought them, and called them, and said: "*Behold Me, behold Me, to a nation that did not call upon My Name*," for they knew it not. "*I have spread forth My hands all the day to an unbelieving people*," the Jews, who would not believe in My word, that I might receive them into My Heart and embrace them in My love. Nor have I done this during one hour only, but all the day long, from the time when I led them out of Egypt in freedom, till My own advent in My Human Nature to visit them; and then from My Birth until My Death upon the Cross.* To the imitation of our Lord in this Ecclesiasticus summons us: "*I will not be ashamed to salute a friend*," because he is of humbler rank,

---

* Isaias lxv. 1.

"*neither will I hide myself from his face*," because he may have done me some injury; "*and if any evil happen to me by him*," because worldly men may ridicule my act, "*I will bear it.*"*

It betokens neither want of self-respect, nor want of spirit, but is an act of true dignity and virtue to be the first to speak kindly to an enemy and try to regain his goodwill, for this is done in imitation of God, on a point which He esteems as intimately connected with His own honour and glory, as He testifies through the Prophet Isaias: "*Therefore the Lord waiteth, that He may have mercy on you.*" He does not summon the sinner at once in the middle of his sins, but bears with and warns him, that He may have an opportunity of sparing him, "*because the Lord is the God of judgment,*" and, being just and true, fulfils His promise by sparing the sinner, who, when thus waited for and called, repents truly of his sin. "*And therefore shall He be exalted, sparing you,*" He shall be magnified and glorified, for that, notwithstanding the sins which a man commits, God's just veracity is declared in His forgiving and showing mercy to those who return to Him. It is then part of the honour and glory of God, and still more is it an honour and glory to a Christian man, that he should imitate God in this, in doing his best to return into favour with one who has injured him, by pardoning him from his heart and asking him to be friends again. All who have acted thus are blessed with much prosperity, and in everything they enjoy the favour of God; while, on the contrary, they who refuse to imitate Him in this, bring down upon themselves the judgments of the Divine wrath, and will have a heavy penalty to pay both in this life and in the next.

There were, as Simeon Metaphrastes relates, two very great friends at Antioch in Syria; one of these was a priest, by name Sapricius, the other a layman, called Nicephorus. These two persons allowed the devil to fan into flame some quarrel between them, which led to the

---

* Ecclus. xxii. 31.

violent severance of their friendship. After a time Nicephorus, bitterly regretting the enmity that had sprung up, paid attentions to Sapricius, and frequently begged him to forgive him. In the persecution set on foot by Valerian and Gallienus, that was then raging, the priest Sapricius was carried off for martyrdom, and had already endured some sufferings in the cause of Christ. While he was being led away to the place of execution, Nicephorus went forward to speak to him, once more begging for his pardon and a renewal of their friendship. The unhappy Sapricius, who had up to this time borne bravely his trials, and had nerved himself for martyrdom, had yet not strength of mind enough to overcome the stubbornness of his temper, and would not yield to the other's petition. On account of this great sin, when he was on the point of suffering death for his faith, by the just judgment of God his strength of purpose failed him, and, renouncing his faith, he incurred the eternal damnation of his soul. Nicephorus, on the other hand, who had with so great earnestness sought reconciliation with his former friend, received such grace from God that, at the same instant, even though unquestioned by the Pagan judge, he boldly vindicated the honour of Christ, and proclaimed himself a Christian, crying out: "I believe in our Lord Jesus Christ, whom this man has renounced." Upon which he received the crown of martyrdom instead.

After this manner does God punish those who refuse to forgive their fellow men, or to be reconciled to an adversary. He allows them to die in their sins, whereas He heaps His favours and His graces on those who ask their enemies to be at peace with them, who humble themselves before them in obedience to the admonition of the Apostle, "*Loving one another with the charity of brotherhood.*"* Nor is it sufficient to do this with the charity of the heart alone —such charity must show itself also in the exterior, "*with honour preventing one another,*" each one striving to be first

* Romans xii. 10.

in marks of respect for the other. And with great reason does the Apostle extend the obligation of mutual love into that of mutual acts of respect, since he who loves does not despise, but esteems the object of his love, and in proportion to the strength of his affection is the fulness of the esteem and consideration that he bears towards him.

CHAPTER LVI.
How we are to exercise towards an enemy the especial charity of conferring benefits on him, and how Christ teaches us to do so by His own example.

THE highest work of the charity by which we should love our enemies, and which indeed embraces every other exercise of it, is to be anxious to benefit them and to be kind to them. This duty comprises some points which are of precept and others which are of counsel. The circumstances which oblige us to do good to a neighbour oblige us also to do good to an enemy, seeing that he too is our neighbour. And these circumstances are, when an enemy stands in need of our assistance, for then, if he is in extreme peril of his soul, we are bound to render him the necessary aid, even at the risk of our lives. If he be in extreme corporal need, the obligation of affording the necessary relief presses on us to the sacrifice of what befits our position in life. If his necessity be not extreme, but only serious, we must come to his aid as far as we can without involving great loss to ourselves. Nor may we exclude our enemies from general acts of kindness; as, for example, in the prayers that we offer up for the faithful, we should include also our enemies. If we are distributing any alms or gifts to others, a just proportion should be assigned to those who may be at variance with us. Beyond such cases as these, the conferring of benefits, or the softening and overcoming them by especial favours, is a work of counsel and perfection.

Upon all these points Scripture instructs us. The Wise Man says: "*If thy enemy be hungry, give him to eat; if he thirst, give him water to drink,*" out of the feeling of charity.* "*For doing this thou shalt heap coals of fire upon his head,*" and so wilt thou convert him from an adversary into a friend.† And God Himself has taught us through Moses: "*If thou meet thy enemy's ox or ass going astray, bring it back to him. If thou seest the ass of him that hateth thee lie underneath his burden, thou shalt not pass by, but shalt lift him up with him.*"‡ These are cases of necessity, in which charity lays an obligation on you.

And Christ, speaking generally of all cases, whether of precept or counsel, says: "*Do good to them that hate you.*"§ And the Apostle: "*Be not overcome by evil*" done you, "*but overcome evil by good;*"‖ for by thus doing good to him you overcome your own wrath, and you overcome your neighbour, for you appease him and bring him to yield himself up to you. You at the same time overcome the devils, since their object in stirring up your neighbour to behave badly towards you, in order to lead you to break the Divine commandment by anger, dissension, and abusive language, you, in refusing to consent to sin, and in increasing charity by showing kindness to an enemy, may thwart, and may thus gain a victory over them, and so may completely "*overcome evil with good.*" Both of this exercise of charity which is of precept and obligatory, and also of that which is of counsel and higher perfection, Jesus Christ our Lord has given us many examples.

Chief of all His enemies was the traitor Judas, and how terrible were the injuries that He received at his hands! And yet our Lord at the Last Supper, though well knowing all the treachery that he had plotted, and the iniquitous compact into which he had entered, would not exclude him from His company, nor deny to him the acts of favour granted to the rest. He admitted him to the

---

* Prov. xxv. 21. † Rom. xii. 20. ‡ Exodus xxiii. 4, 5.
§ St. Matt. v. 44. ‖ Rom. xii. 21.

table along with the other Apostles, He with His own hand helped him from the dish, He administered to him His Sacred Body and Blood, He placed Himself at his feet, and washed and wiped them, and, as some suppose, even kissed them. And as He thus touched his feet He sought to touch also his heart, and tried to soften and win it over by His holy inspirations. The Evangelist, evidently struck with wonder at an act of charity so stupendous, draws attention to the fact: "*The devil having now put into the heart of Judas Iscariot the son of Simon, to betray Him,*" when he had made up his mind to carry out so monstrous a crime as the selling and betraying of our Lord into the power of His enemies, Christ "*putteth water into a basin, and began to wash the feet of the disciples.*"* And when His ungrateful disciple approached at the head of the band sent out to seize Him, He again tried to draw him by kind words, full of wondrous gentleness and charity, to acknowledge and repent of his great crime, thus inviting him back to His friendship. Nay, He even submitted to be kissed by him, and calling him friend, asked "*Whereto art thou come?*"† as though He had said, "Consider what I have done for thee, and what thou hast come to carry out against Me; bethink thee of thy sin, and, repenting of it, turn yet again to Me, for I am ready to forgive thee."

The Chief Priests and Pharisees "*sent ministers to apprehend Jesus,*" that they might put Him to death, and these approached our Lord in the fulfilment of this design. Although they were most wicked men, fully prepared for any crime, and were at this very moment emboldened and excited against Jesus, yet He wrought so merciful a work in them, partly through the words which He addressed to them, partly by the interior graces which He infused into them, that the malice of their hearts was entirely removed, and they were actually changed into faithful disciples and defenders of His truth; for, returning to the Chief Priests they exclaimed: "*Never did man speak*

* St. John xiii. 25.   † St. Matt. xxvi. 50.

like this Man."* Never had they heard such holy doctrine, so admirable and sublime, spoken with such spiritual meaning and efficacy, sinking so deeply into and moving their hearts; never before on earth had they seen or heard the like. Our Lord had bestowed on them a greater benefit, in granting to them this knowledge, esteem, and belief in the truth, than if He had crowned them with dominion over the whole world, for this world would have been but of little value to them, as they would soon have to leave it, but through that faith and fervour of charity He had made them fit for the Kingdom of Heaven—a gift of infinite price and never to have an end.

Again, Malchus had, with greater irreverence and audacity than the rest of our Lord's enemies, pushed forward to lay his hand upon Him and to bind Him, yet as soon as Jesus perceived that he was wounded, and that his right ear had been cut off by a savage blow, He immediately restored this to him, removing at once the pain and disgrace, and leaving him perfectly cured—a benefit so great, that the healing of his body would, had he so willed it, have led to the cure also of his soul. And, inasmuch as he was the servant of the High Priest, our Lord's act was all the more important, for He had not simply healed by miracle a wounded man, but one who was, in addition, an enemy of a dark malignant character, from whom He had already received grievous injury, and was about to receive still more. Another servant of the High Priest, in the presence of his master, with the utmost insolence and cruelty, "*gave Jesus a blow, saying: Answerest Thou the High Priest so?*" for which act he well deserved to be cast down amongst devils, without hope of pardon. Yet here again our Lord was so merciful to him, so full of gentleness, that He at once sought to persuade him to acknowledge and be sorry for his sin: "*If I have spoken evil, give testimony of the evil; but if well, why strikest thou Me?*"† If there be any fault in the words which I have

* St. John vii. 46.   † St. John xviii. 22, 23.

spoken, show wherein it lies; if what I have said is just and true, thou hast struck Me without cause, therefore art thou without excuse, and shouldst be penitent for thy fault.

"We may," says the devout Tauler, "review each incident in the Passion of Christ, but in none shall we find the slightest trace of a movement of anger against His enemies, nor a single indication of indignation in any word, action, or gesture; but rather shall we find every expression of gentleness and sweetness that could possibly have disarmed their malice and converted their hearts. So friendly, so amiable was our Lord, that He made no return to His enemies for the evil they were heaping on Him, except to manifest His love and concern for them."[*] To both Jews and Gentiles, who were the authors of all His torments and the cause of His death, after they had poured forth the whole venom of their hearts upon Him, and the time had come when every creature of God in heaven and on earth might have visited their impiety with the most awful judgments, Jesus displayed a singular mercy, unheard of before—that inanimate creatures, as though endowed with sense, the sun, by darkening its rays, the country round by a terrible earthquake, the rocks torn asunder hither and thither, and the opened sepulchres —should call upon their hearts, that were harder than the very stones, to confess the impiety of which they were guilty, and do penance for it, to implore forgiveness for all their crimes and pray for those graces, those spiritual and heavenly blessings which He had just obtained for them by His death.

To all the sons of Adam—made children of wrath in his fall, and by their own sins become almost without exception the hopeless enemies of God—this Supreme Lord of all creation and Saviour of the whole race of man imparted such priceless benefits as to give His life and shed His blood for them, to offer Himself up to the

[*] Tauler, *De Pass.* cap. xv.

shame and torments of the Cross, and, as far as could be, deliver them all out of sin, making them friends in place of enemies, and instead of being slaves of the devil condemned to eternal flames, raising them to be sons of God and heirs of the Kingdom of Heaven. In order to secure for them this last end—their eternal beatitude—He, during this present life communicates to them the merits of His Passion, most precious gifts of grace, Divine consolations, and other innumerable favours, amongst which are His own most glorious Body for their spiritual food, united, as It is, to His Divinity and seated at the right hand of the Father. These are the benefits which Christ hath conferred on men who are His enemies; and whilst they were in the midst of their hostility against Him, He called, invited, and by His power drew them to the participation of these benefits, disposed and fitted them for their reception.

The Apostle carefully weighed in his mind this unspeakable love of Jesus towards His enemies: "*For why did Christ, when as yet we were weak,*" through the debilitating and deadly effects of sins, "*according to the time*" appointed, "*die for the ungodly?*"* It is as though he said, One of such great majesty could not have undertaken so unwonted an act as to die in behalf of so vile a creature as man, His enemy, except to gain some very important and very certain effect, and this end was that He might give us a sure pledge and hope of eternal glory. And what makes it more wonderful that a God should give His life for wicked and sinful men is, "*that scarce for a just man will one die,*" to save him from evils; not that this is impossible, but very difficult, "*yet perhaps for a good man some one would dare to die,*" and even be willing. But that which Christ did by dying, though so great a Lord, for sinners and enemies, no one else could be found to do, and therefore does it exceed our powers, either of thought or description. Thus powerfully, in

* Romans v. 6, 7.

words that should never be forgotten, does St. Paul explain the greatness of the love of Christ and of the benefits which in His love He has poured forth upon sinners and upon enemies. We are bound to follow in the footsteps and to imitate the example of our Lord and Master, striving to obtain from that same Lord, through our humility, our prayers, and our meditation on His Passion, that true love which reaches to the point of doing good to our enemies and communicating to them real benefits. Let us listen to St. Chrysostom, who, in proposing to us the imitation of Christ, thus exhorts us to this exercise of charity: "Let us draw from Christ Himself this principle of love. He, made truly Man, came to us. He humbled and emptied Himself, and took the form of a servant. He came to dwell amongst the Jewish people, whom He would not leave so long as He remained in mortal flesh; nor did He go into the way of the Gentiles, but traversing the whole country of the Jews, He cured every disease, and healed the complaints of their bodies and souls. They declared that He had a devil, that He blasphemed, and was mad, and was a seducer of the people. But when He heard all this, He so much the more went about doing good, and went forth to meet those who came to crucify Him. And even after He had been crucified, and up to the last breath which He drew, He did everything that He could to save them. Behold, how those ought to be loved who are our enemies, and how we are to copy the example of our Lord."*

* St. Chrysost. *in Ep. ad Ephes.* cap. iv.

CHAPTER LVII.

It behoves us to do good to our enemies in return for the benefit they do us by showing to us our faults and by helping us to correct them.

ALTHOUGH the highest motive for loving and benefiting our enemies is the will of God and the example of Christ our Lord, there remains yet another which should greatly stir us to do the same, and which God Himself puts before us as such a motive. It is that they render a very special help to our souls, and not seldom conduce more to their spiritual life than do our greatest friends. For one of the means towards salvation which man stands most in need of is that his faults and sins should be pointed out to him and corrected, and made to appear to him in all their real baseness, in order that he may feel and deplore them; seeing that, from the passion of self-love which so much blinds him, he will not acknowledge to himself many sins that he commits, and those that he does confess to, he does not duly weigh nor make up his mind to correct them. It is but seldom in this world that one can find friends who will help him in this need; nay, friends too often conceal the truth, hide the faults of one whom they love, and flatter him, praising much of the evil which he does, making light of many of his defects, and exaggerating whatever good they find in him. Since they wish to maintain their friendship with him, and turn it as much as possible to their own account, they do not venture to chide him in anything which they know will vex him, however necessary it may be for his good. They only say that to him which will please him, though they know well it is injurious to his soul. Hence one who is accounted a friend, really acts to us the part of an enemy, as the Wise Man warns us: *"A man that speaketh to his friend with flattering and dissembling words, spreadeth a net for his feet."* *

Wherefore God, seeing this very marked deficiency in acknowledged friends as regards a point of so great moment and so nearly affecting our salvation, permits that we should have enemies who will render us the required service. These take note of and expose their neighbours' faults in their real deformity, holding them to be their enemies, and reproaching them for their delinquencies. They are not friends who lay in wait for you, closely watch you, and thus turn you aside from many dangerous occasions to your soul, making you afraid to do wrong. May then these your enemies be watchful and active in detecting all you say or do, lest you neglect yourself, but, on the contrary, may learn to fear not merely that which is evil, but that also which might cause suspicion, or wear the appearance of evil, may they fill you with the dread of sinning to avoid the possibility of their speaking ill of you, or spreading any report against you, or of accusing you before any one who is likely, or who may be bound to punish you. Thus enemies are like timepieces, keeping their neighbours' lives well ordered and regulated, or they are like guardians and most vigilant tutors, who keep their eyes always fixed on them; and in this way they are far more useful to us than friends. Whence St. Chrysostom says: "That usefulness which friends fail to afford us, our enemies confer upon us."† And St. Augustine supplies the cause of this when he writes: "As friends injure us by their adulation, so our enemies, by finding fault with us and speaking ill of us, very generally lead to our correction."‡ And though our enemies in thus telling the truth of us and helping to correct our faults, by no means wish

---

* Prov. xxix. 5.   † St. Chrysost. hom. iii. *De David et Saul.*
‡ St. Aug. *Confess.* lib. ix. cap. viii.

us any good, it is not the less certain that God wishes our good, and makes use of them as an instrument to promote it. For it is in this way that the Divine Providence generally works, drawing good out of evil, and transforming evil into good. It is also the part of Divine predestination to direct and control all events for the salvation of the elect. And in order to regard this in the light of a great benefit, so as to love our enemies and be ready to oblige them, it is enough that we know that God thus regards it, Who has bid us love our enemies, and that we are bound to please Him in this; and also that God enjoins on us to love and do good to our enemies out of a feeling of gratitude for the benefit which through them He confers on us.

We should likewise be very diligent in gathering fruit from this favour which God does us in the person of our enemies, listening attentively to all that they say of us, and weighing it carefully without the slightest spirit of self-love. And whatever of real fault we detect in ourselves, let us weep over it with heartfelt sorrow, and confessing it in the presence of God and of His servant, let us humble ourselves and amend. Our minds need not revert to the uncharitable intention of an enemy in telling this unfavourable truth concerning us, let us look only at the holy and most loving design of God, as though it was His mouth which had spoken it. Were a man, imprisoned in some tower, to be dying of hunger, he would most thankfully grasp hold of and begin to eat the loaves that an enemy might hurl at his face in order to injure him, and would pay little attention to the ill-will of his assailant, but think only of his own hunger and of the good providence of God which had sent these loaves to him. So, when an enemy tells you of your faults and this humbles you, regard not his bad intention in the matter, but reflect on the great good this injury and shame will be to you, if only, being thus led to acknowledge what is is wrong, you humble yourself and amend, and if it purifies you through the very pain that it causes. Wherefore you ought to accept and embrace this as a gift from God and as most wholesome food for your soul, from which you should profit; for in truth, says St. Basil, "tribulations are a sort of meat of the soul, a training that helps wonderfully to root out vices and nurture virtue, and make the spiritual combatant more deserving of the glory of God." *

These, then, are the acts of charity which we are bound to perform towards our enemies. We must remove from them all cause of anger, we must bear patiently with them, rejoice in their good, sympathize in their misfortunes; we may not discontinue the good that before we did them, nor the ordinary intercourse and civility due to them, but even ourselves confer benefits on them. In this way shall we greatly please God, as David did under the Old Law, so that God pronounced this of him: "*The Lord hath sought Him a man according to His own Heart.*"† And St. Stephen and all the other saints of the New Testament also greatly pleased Him because they felt such love for and bestowed such benefits on their enemies. We shall find, too, our prayers most efficacious to obtain all that we desire of Him, for thus was it with Moses and Samuel, and with innumerable martyrs and confessors of the New Law, who prayed for their enemies with the most fervent desire of their hearts. Nay, as true sons, we shall resemble our Lord and Saviour Jesus Christ, imitating Him in that which He Himself, as Man, did and suffered for His enemies. We shall share in all His merits and gifts without measure, for these are poured forth all the more abundantly in proportion as we copy Him the more closely.

Moreover thus shall we achieve more glorious victories, since in loving and benefiting our enemies we are conquering ourselves, we are triumphing over our passions, our anger, our feeling of sadness, our self-love, subjecting these

* St. Basil, *Psal.* xxxiii. † 1 Kings xiii. 14.

to right reason and to the Divine will. Besides which we conquer our enemies themselves, by appeasing them, by conciliating them, by removing their anger and ill-will, and changing them into friends. Lastly, we are victorious over the very devils, and overwhelm them with confusion. By these signal conquests we become an object of admiration to the world, we edify the Church by the example of our exalted charity, we fill the angels with delight, we actually increase the glory of God, and through His grace we render ourselves more worthy to enter into His eternal glory.

THE END.

www.ingramcontent.com/pod-product-compliance
Lightning Source LLC
Chambersburg PA
CBHW021821230426
43669CB00008B/826